THE ULTIMATE
FIFTH GRADE
MATH WORKBOOK

ISBN: 9781947569454
27 26 25 24 23 10 11 12 13 14

Printed in China

Let's Learn!

Numbers are made up of digits. The **value** of each digit depends on its **place**. You can use a place value chart to find the place and value of each digit. For example, look at the chart for 4,862,915 below.

Millions		Hundred thousands	Ten thousands	Thousands		Hundreds	Tens	Ones
4	,	8	6	2	,	9	1	5

Circle the digit in the thousands place.

(5),448   3,481,966   23,481   178,931

Circle the digit in the ten-thousands place.

228,384   6,484,281   2,234,725   48,276

Circle the digit in the hundred-thousands place.

7,285,395   948,285   164,481   2,528,947

IXL.com skill ID Y7Q

For more practice, visit IXL.com or the IXL mobile app and enter this code in the search bar.

Write each number in standard form.

5,000 + 900 + 40 + 5   _____5,945_____

70,000 + 300 + 20 + 5   _____

600,000 + 70,000 + 6,000 + 80   _____

400,000 + 90,000 + 500 + 20 + 9   _____

300,000 + 5,000 + 100 + 70 + 3   _____

2,000,000 + 50,000 + 700 + 8   _____

Write each number in expanded form.

56,710   ___50,000 + 6,000 + 700 + 10___

260,017   _____

184,005   _____

4,095,800   _____

9,560,000   _____

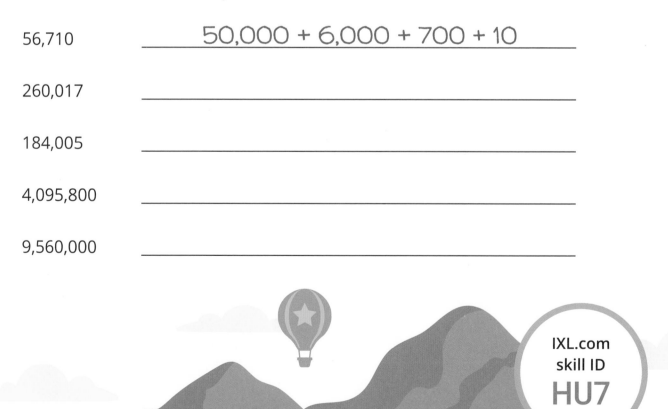

Match each number to its name.

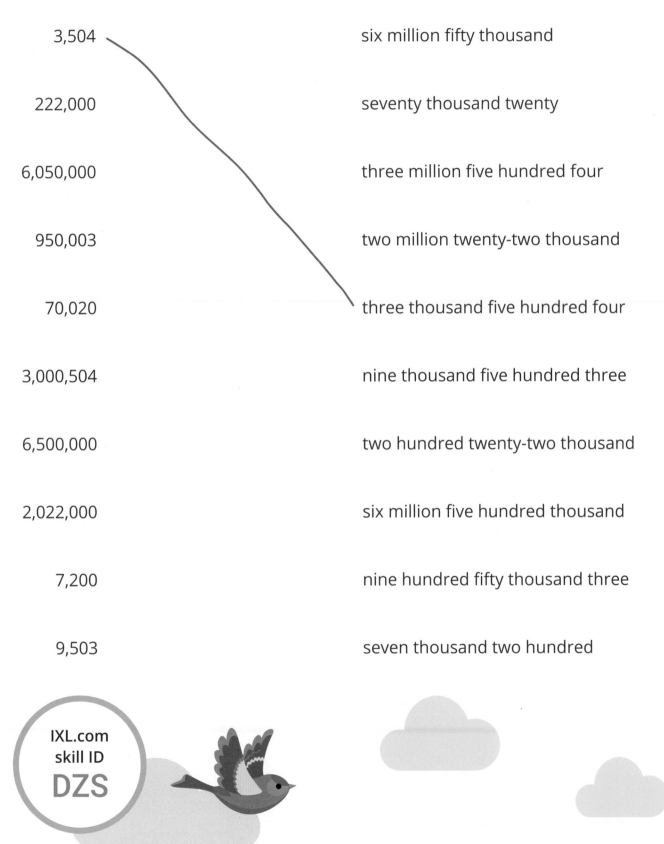

3,504	six million fifty thousand
222,000	seventy thousand twenty
6,050,000	three million five hundred four
950,003	two million twenty-two thousand
70,020	three thousand five hundred four
3,000,504	nine thousand five hundred three
6,500,000	two hundred twenty-two thousand
2,022,000	six million five hundred thousand
7,200	nine hundred fifty thousand three
9,503	seven thousand two hundred

Let's Learn!

The places in a number are related to each other. Each place is 10 times as much as the place to its right.

×10	×10	×10	×10	×10	×10

Millions	Hundred thousands	Ten thousands	Thousands	Hundreds	Tens	Ones

You can use this pattern to find the relationship between different numbers. Look at the examples below.

3,000 is 10 times as much as 300.

500 is 10 times as much as 50.

Use the place value pattern to fill in the missing numbers.

___80,000___ is 10 times as much as 8,000.

400 is 10 times as much as _____.

_____ is 10 times as much as 500.

2,000,000 is 10 times as much as _____.

_____ is 10 times as much as 7.

300,000 is 10 times as much as _____.

IXL.com
skill ID
KFD

Compare each pair of numbers using > or <.

7,171   <   7,711

53,385 ◯ 5,385

2,473 ◯ 23,474

1,618 ◯ 16,180

67,817 ◯ 67,717

59,926 ◯ 599,926

613,240 ◯ 61,324

1,221,122 ◯ 1,121,122

750,004 ◯ 570,004

3,444,924 ◯ 3,444,927

100,001 ◯ 100,010

9,005,757 ◯ 9,500,700

IXL.com
skill ID
CLB

Write the numbers in order from least to greatest.

7,148   7,841   7,418

__7,148__   __7,418__   __7,841__

44,480   40,884   41,884

_____   _____   _____

68,963   6,893   686,933

_____   _____   _____

557,727   575,727   552,777

_____   _____   _____

4,989,119   4,988,991   4,988,919

_____   _____   _____

Let's Learn!

When you multiply by multiples of 10, you can use patterns with zeros! Look at the examples below. First, multiply the non-zero parts. Then, add on the total number of zeros in your answer.

$5 \times 700 = 3,500$ 　　0 zeros + 2 zeros = 2 zeros

$30 \times 400 = 12,000$ 　　1 zero + 2 zeros = 3 zeros

Multiply.

$9 \times 400 =$ ___3,600___　　　　$40 \times 80 =$ ___3,200___

$20 \times 90 =$ _____　　　　$3 \times 500 =$ _____

$6 \times 400 =$ _____　　　　$30 \times 200 =$ _____

$3 \times 6,000 =$ _____　　　　$2 \times 7,000 =$ _____

$2 \times 80,000 =$ _____　　　　$600 \times 70 =$ _____

IXL.com
skill ID
BCK

Keep going! Multiply.

50 × 500 = _____

700 × 10 = _____

6 × 60,000 = _____

300 × 800 = _____

800 × 700 = _____

5 × 11,000 = _____

4 × 20,000 = _____

9 × 10,000 = _____

300 × 1,000 = _____

7 × 300,000 = _____

9 × 70,000 = _____

400 × 5,000 = _____

8 × 8,000,000 = _____

9,000 × 600 = _____

5,000 × 800 = _____

90 × 800,000 = _____

Let's Learn!

You can also use multiples of 10 to **estimate** products. Try it with 38 × 72.
Round each factor to the nearest 10. Then multiply to find an estimate.

38 × 72 is about 40 × 70 = 2,800

Estimate by rounding each factor.

22 × 38 is about ___20___ × ___40___ = ___800___

31 × 33 is about _____ × _____ = _____

17 × 72 is about _____ × _____ = _____

88 × 42 is about _____ × _____ = _____

49 × 58 is about _____ × _____ = _____

62 × 29 is about _____ × _____ = _____

78 × 51 is about _____ × _____ = _____

89 × 79 is about _____ × _____ = _____

IXL.com
skill ID
TKD

Use the distributive property to multiply. Follow the example.

$4 \times 82 =$ _____328_____

$4 \times (80 + 2)$

$(4 \times 80) + (4 \times 2)$

$320 + 8 = 328$

$7 \times 34 =$ _____

$8 \times 56 =$ _____

$3 \times 96 =$ _____

$2 \times 87 =$ _____

$5 \times 41 =$ _____

$6 \times 79 =$ _____

$9 \times 68 =$ _____

IXL.com
skill ID
6PN

Keep going! Use the distributive property to multiply.

7 × 235 = ___1,645___

7 × (200 + 30 + 5)
(7 × 200) + (7 × 30) + (7 × 5)
1,400 + 210 + 35 = 1,645

4 × 128 = _____

8 × 373 = _____

6 × 299 = _____

5 × 567 = _____

3 × 948 = _____

9 × 726 = _____

7 × 679 = _____

Boost your math learning and save 20%!

Scan this QR code for details.

Multiply.

```
  2
  3 7                    2 9                  1 4 5
×   4                  ×   6                ×     5
─────                  ─────                ───────
1 4 8
```

```
  3 8 1                  7 2 6                  8 0 8
×     9                ×     3                ×     2
───────                ───────                ───────
```

```
  5 7 7                  6 3 9                  9 8 4
×     8                ×     7                ×     9
───────                ───────                ───────
```

```
1 , 0 5 8              3 , 4 5 0              1 , 7 8 3
×       3              ×       4              ×       6
─────────              ─────────              ─────────
```

Multiply.

$$
\begin{array}{r}
\scriptstyle 1 \\
3\,4 \\
\times\,2\,3 \\
\hline
1\,0\,2 \\
+\,6\,8\,0 \\
\hline
7\,8\,2
\end{array}
\qquad
\begin{array}{r}
2\,8 \\
\times\,1\,1 \\
\hline
\end{array}
\qquad
\begin{array}{r}
5\,2 \\
\times\,3\,8 \\
\hline
\end{array}
$$

$$
\begin{array}{r}
3\,0 \\
\times\,7\,9 \\
\hline
\end{array}
\qquad
\begin{array}{r}
6\,4 \\
\times\,5\,6 \\
\hline
\end{array}
\qquad
\begin{array}{r}
7\,2 \\
\times\,2\,7 \\
\hline
\end{array}
$$

$$
\begin{array}{r}
8\,8 \\
\times\,4\,4 \\
\hline
\end{array}
\qquad
\begin{array}{r}
7\,6 \\
\times\,9\,1 \\
\hline
\end{array}
\qquad
\begin{array}{r}
4\,5 \\
\times\,8\,3 \\
\hline
\end{array}
$$

Two-digit by three-digit multiplication

Keep going! Multiply.

$$112 \times 23$$

$$368 \times 14$$

$$454 \times 32$$

$$509 \times 47$$

$$719 \times 22$$

$$346 \times 56$$

$$595 \times 58$$

$$738 \times 63$$

$$827 \times 85$$

$$642 \times 79$$

$$434 \times 94$$

$$763 \times 88$$

IXL.com
skill ID
JHB

Multiply.

$$
\begin{array}{r}
1,531 \\
\times \quad 25 \\
\hline
\end{array}
\qquad
\begin{array}{r}
3,174 \\
\times \quad 43 \\
\hline
\end{array}
\qquad
\begin{array}{r}
2,820 \\
\times \quad 35 \\
\hline
\end{array}
$$

$$
\begin{array}{r}
1,898 \\
\times \quad 17 \\
\hline
\end{array}
\qquad
\begin{array}{r}
7,118 \\
\times \quad 50 \\
\hline
\end{array}
\qquad
\begin{array}{r}
5,055 \\
\times \quad 26 \\
\hline
\end{array}
$$

$$
\begin{array}{r}
2,787 \\
\times \quad 49 \\
\hline
\end{array}
\qquad
\begin{array}{r}
3,118 \\
\times \quad 89 \\
\hline
\end{array}
\qquad
\begin{array}{r}
5,718 \\
\times \quad 77 \\
\hline
\end{array}
$$

$$
\begin{array}{r}
4,510 \\
\times \quad 76 \\
\hline
\end{array}
\qquad
\begin{array}{r}
9,628 \\
\times \quad 87 \\
\hline
\end{array}
$$

IXL.com
skill ID
9VQ

Multiply to complete the crossword puzzle.

ACROSS

3. 2 3 7
      × 6 4

4. 1 1 5
      × 4 2

6. 7 3 2
      × 6 3

DOWN

1. 7 3
      × 3 5

2. 4 , 6 5 8
      ×   5 6

5. 2 2 8
      × 2 8

7. 1 , 1 5 6
      ×   1 7

Multiply. Compare each pair of products using >, <, or =.

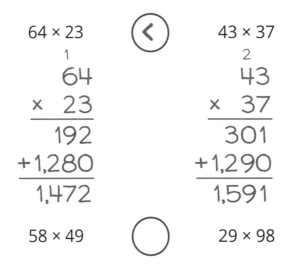

$$64 \times 23 \quad < \quad 43 \times 37$$

$$
\begin{array}{r}
\overset{1}{6}4 \\
\times \quad 23 \\
\hline
192 \\
+1{,}280 \\
\hline
1{,}472
\end{array}
\qquad
\begin{array}{r}
\overset{2}{4}3 \\
\times \quad 37 \\
\hline
301 \\
+1{,}290 \\
\hline
1{,}591
\end{array}
$$

$$58 \times 49 \quad \bigcirc \quad 29 \times 98$$

$$499 \times 33 \quad \bigcirc \quad 504 \times 28$$

$$1{,}794 \times 67 \quad \bigcirc \quad 2{,}316 \times 52$$

Answer each question.

Lindsey sells jars of fruit jam at the farmers' market. She includes 3 jars of jam in a pack, and she has 26 packs at her stand. How many jars of jam does she have at her stand?

_____

At Sunrise Bakery, the baker uses large pans that each hold 24 muffins. How many muffins can he make using 16 large pans?

_____

A plane flies at an average speed of 494 miles per hour. At this speed, how many miles will the plane fly in 5 hours?

_____

Center Stage Drama Club sold 178 tickets to its annual talent show. Each ticket cost $12. How much money did the drama club earn from ticket sales?

_____

A car company builds a truck that weighs 3,977 pounds. How much do 25 trucks weigh?

_____

IXL.com
skill ID
J95

Answer each question.

Georgetown Skating Rink held a public skating session on Saturday. They sold 78 adult tickets for $8 each and 129 children's tickets for $6 each. How much money did the rink make in all?

_____

Jeff takes the train from Boston to Baltimore. The route is 416 miles long one-way. If Jeff goes to Baltimore and back 3 times, how many miles will he travel?

_____

Izzy's Craft Studio offers necklace-making classes. There are 3 classes each week, with 28 students in each class. Each student is given 50 beads to make a necklace. How many total beads are given out each week?

_____

Mr. Aiken gave his class a reading challenge last week. The students could pick between two books: a 225-page novel or a 198-page book of short stories. If 18 students read the novel and 12 students read the book of short stories, how many total pages did the class read?

_____

Let's Learn!

When dividing with multiples of 10, you can use division facts and patterns with zeros! Look at the examples below. Start by looking for a basic division fact. Then subtract to find the total number of zeros in your answer.

$2,400 \div 8 = 300$ 2 zeros – 0 zeros = 2 zeros

$36,000 \div 60 = 600$ 3 zeros – 1 zero = 2 zeros

Divide.

$18,000 \div 6 =$ ___3,000___

$56,000 \div 80 =$ ___700___

$48,000 \div 8 =$ _____

$30,000 \div 6 =$ _____

$2,700 \div 30 =$ _____

$280,000 \div 7 =$ _____

$500,000 \div 5 =$ _____

$64,000 \div 80 =$ _____

$350,000 \div 7 =$ _____

$2,000 \div 50 =$ _____

$490,000 \div 70 =$ _____

$110,000 \div 11 =$ _____

IXL.com
skill ID
8Z6

Keep going! Divide.

1,800,000 ÷ 9 = _____

3,200,000 ÷ 80 = _____

1,000,000 ÷ 10 = _____

4,800,000 ÷ 12 = _____

3,000,000 ÷ 5 = _____

140,000 ÷ 70 = _____

720,000 ÷ 60 = _____

600,000 ÷ 12 = _____

200,000 ÷ 20 = _____

8,100,000 ÷ 90 = _____

200,000 ÷ 40 = _____

4,000,000 ÷ 50 = _____

3,600,000 ÷ 40 = _____

IXL.com
skill ID
J8Y

Divide.

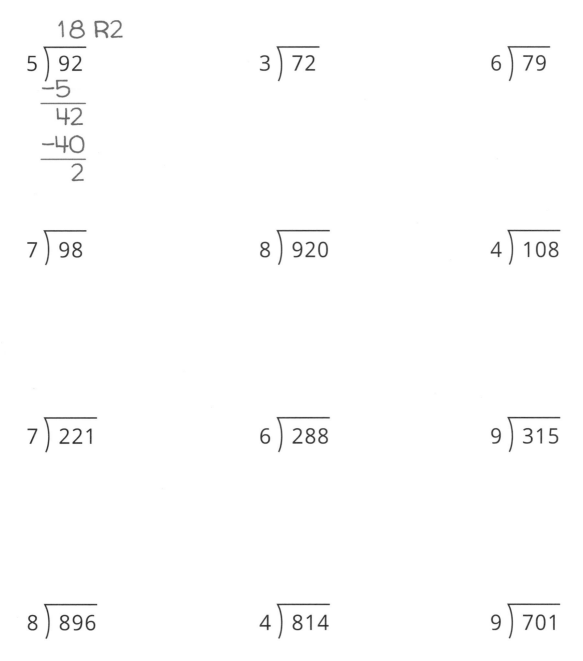

$$5 \overline{)92} \quad \begin{array}{c} 18\ R2 \\ \hline \end{array}$$
$$-5$$
$$\overline{42}$$
$$-40$$
$$\overline{2}$$

$$3 \overline{)72}$$

$$6 \overline{)79}$$

$$7 \overline{)98}$$

$$8 \overline{)920}$$

$$4 \overline{)108}$$

$$7 \overline{)221}$$

$$6 \overline{)288}$$

$$9 \overline{)315}$$

$$8 \overline{)896}$$

$$4 \overline{)814}$$

$$9 \overline{)701}$$

TAKE ANOTHER LOOK! How can you use multiplication to check your work on this page? Try it for one of the problems!

Divide.

$3\overline{)947}$ $\qquad$ $8\overline{)488}$ $\qquad$ $6\overline{)444}$

$9\overline{)936}$ $\qquad$ $7\overline{)718}$ $\qquad$ $5\overline{)1,280}$

$8\overline{)3,228}$ $\qquad$ $9\overline{)2,583}$ $\qquad$ $6\overline{)1,536}$

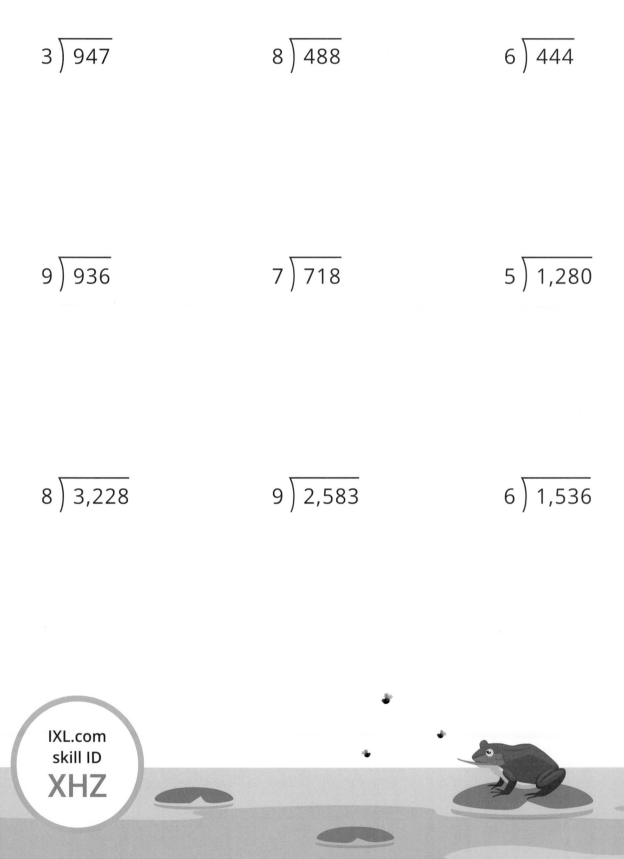

Divide.

737 ÷ 3 = __245 R2__

```
      245 R2
3 ) 737
   -6
   ___
    13
   -12
   ___
    17
   -15
   ___
     2
```

912 ÷ 8 = _____

2,322 ÷ 6 = _____

2,209 ÷ 4 = _____

Answer each question.

Gabriel sells homemade dog treats. He made 184 dog treats and wants to put 4 in each bag. How many bags of dog treats can he make?

_____

Mandie works at a bookstore, and she helps set up for events. For a book signing, she set up 108 chairs into 6 equal rows. How many chairs are in each row?

_____

Kyle saved the same amount of money each month for 9 months. How much did he save each month if he saved a total of $3,915?

_____

The fifth graders at Erica's school went bowling. There were 142 students on the trip. If 6 students could bowl on each lane, how many lanes did they need for all of the students? How many students bowled on the lane that was not full?

_____

Let's Learn!

You can use division facts and multiples of 10 to estimate quotients.

Try it with 489 ÷ 6. Think about the nearby multiples of 10 that you can divide by 6. Those numbers are 480 and 540. Since 489 is closer to 480, use that number to estimate.

489 ÷ 6
↓
480 ÷ 6 = 80

So, 489 ÷ 6 is close to 80.

Estimate each quotient.

158 ÷ 8 is close to __20__.
↓
160 ÷ 8 = 20

263 ÷ 9 is close to _____.

368 ÷ 7 is close to _____.

104 ÷ 5 is close to _____.

371 ÷ 6 is close to _____.

651 ÷ 9 is close to _____.

719 ÷ 8 is close to _____.

355 ÷ 4 is close to _____.

Let's Learn!

You can estimate with larger divisors, too! Think about 87 ÷ 21. You will need to change both numbers to estimate. Choose nearby multiples of 10 to make the division easier. You can rewrite the problem as 80 ÷ 20.

$$87 ÷ 21$$
$$↓ \quad ↓$$
$$80 ÷ 20 = 4$$

So, 87 ÷ 21 is close to 4.

Estimate each quotient.

64 ÷ 31 is close to ___2___.

$$60 ÷ 30 = 2$$

57 ÷ 29 is close to _____.

83 ÷ 41 is close to _____.

73 ÷ 18 is close to _____.

98 ÷ 19 is close to _____.

65 ÷ 22 is close to _____.

Let's Learn!

You can also estimate problems like 161 ÷ 32. As before, choose nearby multiples of 10 to make the division easier.

161 ÷ 32

150 ÷ 30 = 5

So, 161 ÷ 32 is close to 5.

Estimate each quotient.

638 ÷ 79 is close to ___8___.

640 ÷ 80 = 8

551 ÷ 61 is close to _____.

253 ÷ 42 is close to _____.

368 ÷ 53 is close to _____.

111 ÷ 27 is close to _____.

442 ÷ 88 is close to _____.

IXL.com
skill ID
EFW

Let's Learn!

You can use long division to divide by two-digit numbers. You may need to use estimation to help. Try it for 787 ÷ 19.

```
      41 R8
19 ) 787
    −76
     27
   − 19
      8
```

To start, you will need to find out how many times 19 goes into 78. Estimate by changing 78 to 80 and 19 to 20. Since 80 ÷ 20 = 4, try 4 as the first digit of the quotient.

Now, follow the steps for long division to solve.

So, 787 ÷ 19 = 41 R8.

Divide.

```
      12
29 ) 348
   −29
    58
   −58
     0
```

22) 475

27) 621

21) 663

31) 682

18) 972

Divide.

$46\overline{)552}$ $22\overline{)687}$ $19\overline{)574}$

$21\overline{)882}$ $28\overline{)912}$ $82\overline{)904}$

$35\overline{)779}$ $28\overline{)646}$ $13\overline{)1,456}$

$17\overline{)2,414}$ $28\overline{)5,634}$

IXL.com
skill ID
HMA

Let's Learn!

For some division problems, you may need to estimate with larger numbers. Try it for 1,474 ÷ 67.

```
        22
 67 ) 1,474
     -134
      134
     -134
        0
```

To start, estimate how many times 67 goes into 147. Change 67 to 70 and 147 to 140. Since 140 ÷ 70 = 2, try 2 as the first digit of the quotient.

Now, complete the long division to solve.

So, 1,474 ÷ 67 = 22.

Divide.

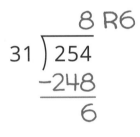

```
       8 R6
 31 ) 254
     -248
        6
```

28) 159

31) 218

29) 174

32) 2,241

27) 1,701

Divide.

$19 \overline{)1{,}425}$ $32 \overline{)1{,}314}$ $27 \overline{)1{,}221}$

$42 \overline{)1{,}263}$ $17 \overline{)1{,}001}$ $28 \overline{)1{,}980}$

$36 \overline{)1{,}191}$ $38 \overline{)3{,}116}$ $41 \overline{)1{,}271}$

$18 \overline{)1{,}152}$ $53 \overline{)1{,}601}$

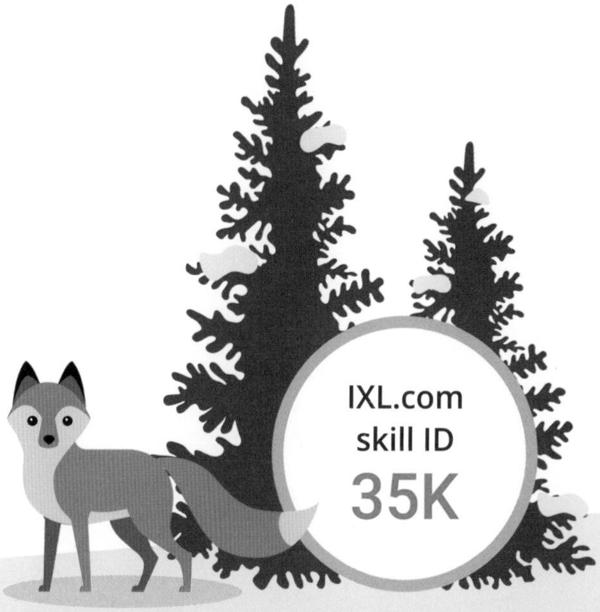

IXL.com
skill ID
35K

Let's Learn!

When you estimate during long division, sometimes your estimate might be a little off. When that happens, you will need to adjust the quotient. Try it with 1,568 ÷ 33.

$$\begin{array}{r} 5 \\ 33 \overline{)\, 1,568} \\ -\,165 \end{array}$$

If you change 33 to 30 and 156 to 150, you would think the first digit of the quotient is 5. Try 5 as the first digit. Since you can't subtract 165 from 156, the estimate of 5 was too high.

$$\begin{array}{r} 47 \text{ R17} \\ 33 \overline{)\, 1,568} \\ -\,132 \\ \hline 248 \\ -\,231 \\ \hline 17 \end{array}$$

Since the estimate was too high, try placing 4 as the first digit. Then keep dividing to solve.

So, 1,568 ÷ 33 = 47 R17.

If your estimate is too low, adjust the quotient to the next higher number. Try it with 678 ÷ 16.

$$\begin{array}{r} 3 \\ 16 \overline{)\, 678} \\ -\,48 \\ \hline 19 \end{array}$$

If you change 16 to 20 and 67 to 60, you would think the first digit of the quotient is 3. When you try 3, there are 19 left over. Since 19 is bigger than 16, your estimate was too low.

$$\begin{array}{r} 42 \text{ R6} \\ 16 \overline{)\, 678} \\ -\,64 \\ \hline 38 \\ -\,32 \\ \hline 6 \end{array}$$

Try 4. Using long division, you will find that 678 ÷ 16 = 42 R6.

Divide.

$21 \overline{)588}$

$17 \overline{)153}$

$39 \overline{)311}$

$29 \overline{)841}$

$64 \overline{)530}$

$34 \overline{)942}$

$42 \overline{)2,294}$

$58 \overline{)2,262}$

$93 \overline{)1,825}$

Keep going! Divide.

$43 \overline{)818}$ $19 \overline{)722}$ $46 \overline{)414}$

$31 \overline{)1,922}$ $37 \overline{)1,519}$ $84 \overline{)3,870}$

$29 \overline{)2,639}$ $28 \overline{)1,179}$ $34 \overline{)1,033}$

Answer each question.

Avery played a treasure hunt game on her tablet. She earned 36 bonus points each time she found a hidden treasure box. How many treasure boxes did she find if she earned 612 bonus points?

_____

Pete owns a pet store. The store has 432 fish and 18 aquariums. Pete wants to put the same number of fish in each aquarium. How many fish should he put in each aquarium?

_____

Teddy pays for a music streaming service every month. He pays a total of $192 per year. How much does he pay each month?

_____

Callie's Restaurant is moving to a new location. The movers are packing drinking glasses into boxes that hold 18 glasses each. There are 350 glasses that need to be packed. How many boxes will be full? How many glasses will be in the box that's not full?

_____

Time to review! Solve.

674 × 3 = _____

188 ÷ 5 = _____

408 ÷ 6 = _____

4 × 1,259 = _____

2,116 ÷ 9 = _____

88 × 17 = _____

36 × 52 = _____

674 ÷ 21 = _____

Keep going! Solve.

$145 \div 18 =$ _____

$17 \times 296 =$ _____

$4{,}329 \times 66 =$ _____

$6{,}300 \div 28 =$ _____

$5{,}547 \times 79 =$ _____

$8{,}558 \div 19 =$ _____

$7{,}106 \div 34 =$ _____

$1{,}735 \div 36 =$ _____

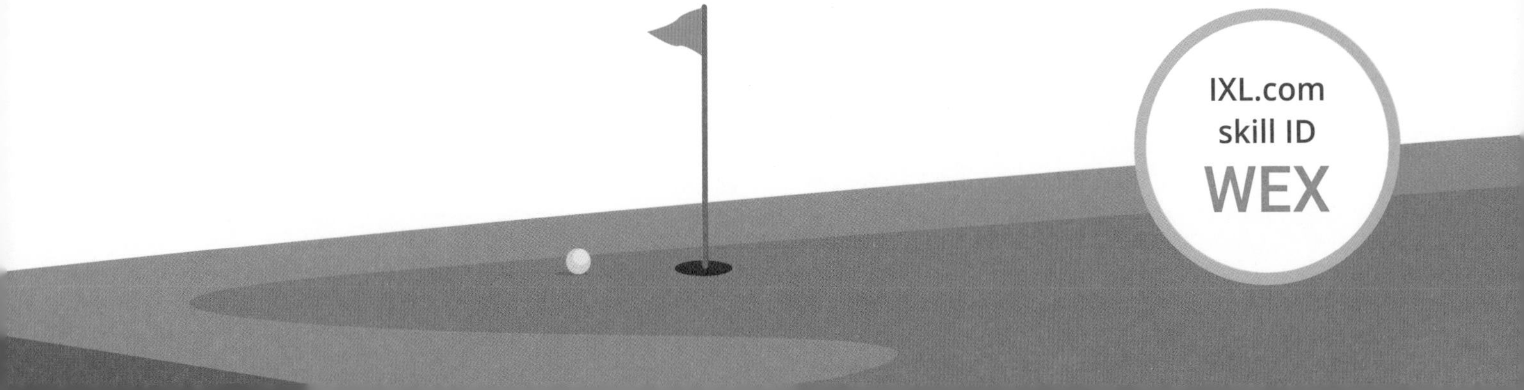

Follow the path from start to finish.

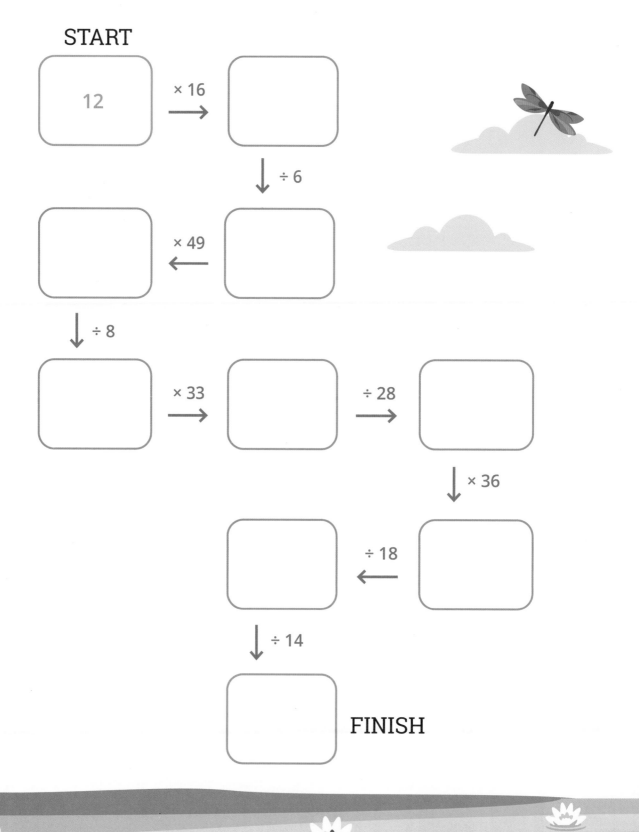

START

12 × 16 →

↓ ÷ 6

← × 49

↓ ÷ 8

× 33 → ÷ 28 →

↓ × 36

÷ 18 ←

↓ ÷ 14

FINISH

Let's Learn!

When you multiply the same number over and over, you can write the problem using an **exponent**! Look at the examples. The small numbers are exponents, and they show how many 7s are in each expression.

$7 = 7^1$

$7 \times 7 = 7^2$

$7 \times 7 \times 7 = 7^3$

$7 \times 7 \times 7 \times 7 = 7^4$

Rewrite each expression using an exponent.

$8 \times 8 \times 8 \times 8 \times 8 \times 8 \times 8 = \underline{8^7}$

$9 \times 9 \times 9 = \underline{\hspace{2cm}}$

$3 \times 3 \times 3 \times 3 \times 3 \times 3 = \underline{\hspace{2cm}}$

$10 \times 10 = \underline{\hspace{2cm}}$

$12 \times 12 = \underline{\hspace{2cm}}$

$78 \times 78 \times 78 \times 78 = \underline{\hspace{2cm}}$

$45 \times 45 \times 45 \times 45 \times 45 = \underline{\hspace{2cm}}$

$2 \times 2 \times 2 \times 2 \times 2 \times 2 \times 2 \times 2 = \underline{\hspace{2cm}}$

Rewrite each expression in expanded form.

$9^5 = \underline{9 \times 9 \times 9 \times 9 \times 9}$

$18^1 = \underline{\hspace{3cm}}$

$31^3 = \underline{\hspace{3cm}}$

$2^6 = \underline{\hspace{3cm}}$

$55^2 = \underline{\hspace{3cm}}$

$44^4 = \underline{\hspace{3cm}}$

$72^5 = \underline{\hspace{3cm}}$

$8^6 = \underline{\hspace{3cm}}$

Find the value of each expression.

$4^2 =$ _____ 4 × 4 = 16 _____ $7^2 =$ _____

$10^3 =$ _____ $12^2 =$ _____

$8^1 =$ _____ $9^3 =$ _____

$11^2 =$ _____ $17^2 =$ _____

Compare the value of the expressions using >, <, or =.

8^2 $\left(>\right)$ 16^1 9^1 $\bigcirc$ 3^2 5^3 $\bigcirc$ 10^2

64 > 16

13^2 $\bigcirc$ 26^1 14^2 $\bigcirc$ 7^3 64^1 $\bigcirc$ 4^3

IXL.com
skill ID
XFF

Exploration Zone

EXPONENTS WITH 10

There is a special pattern when you use exponents with 10. Look at the table. What pattern do you notice? Can you use this pattern to fill in the table?

Exponents with 10			
10^1	10	10	1 zero
10^2	10 × 10	100	2 zeros
10^3	10 × 10 × 10	1,000	3 zeros
10^4	10 × 10 × 10 × 10		
10^5			
10^6			

TRY IT YOURSELF!

Use the pattern to solve.

$10^7 = $ ___10,000,000___

$10^8 = $ _____

$10^9 = $ _____

$10^{10} = $ _____

Keep it going! How many zeros will 10^{32} have? How about 10^{91}?

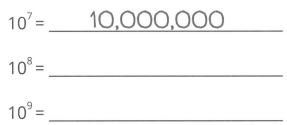

IXL.com
skill ID
KGQ

Let's Learn!

To simplify an expression with multiple operations, you must follow the **order of operations:**

1. Parentheses
2. Exponents
3. Multiplication and division, from left to right
4. Addition and subtraction, from left to right

If your problem doesn't have one of these steps, move on to the next one. Try it! Use the order of operations to solve $3 + 5 \times 2 - (4 + 1)$.

$3 + 5 \times 2 - (4 + 1)$	First, simplify what's inside the parentheses: $4 + 1 = 5$.
$3 + 5 \times 2 - 5$	Then, multiply $5 \times 2 = 10$.
$3 + 10 - 5$	Then, add $3 + 10 = 13$.
$13 - 5 = 8$	Finally, subtract $13 - 5$ to get the answer, 8.

Simplify using the order of operations.

$20 \div (1 + 4) = \underline{\quad 4 \quad}$

$20 \div 5 = 4$

$3^2 + 4 = \underline{\quad 13 \quad}$

$9 + 4 = 13$

$14 - 6 \div 2 = \underline{\qquad\qquad}$

$33 - 12 + 4^2 = \underline{\qquad\qquad}$

$(7 + 3) \times (15 - 12) = \underline{\qquad\qquad}$

$15 + (54 \div 9 - 2) + 10 = \underline{\qquad\qquad}$

Simplify using the order of operations.

$25 \times 2 \div 5 - 8 =$ _____

$(4 + 32) \div 6 \times 2 =$ _____

$27 \div (45 - 36) + 3 =$ _____

$16 + 6^2 - 4 \div 2 =$ _____

$9^2 - 12 \times 2 \div 6 =$ _____

$35 \div (12 - 5) + 10 \times 7 =$ _____

$44 - 12 \times 2 + 5 \times 15 =$ _____

$72 \div (4 + 15 - 7) =$ _____

Compare each pair of expressions using >, <, or =.

$$7 + 4 - 3 \times 2 \quad \boxed{<} \quad 7 + (4 - 3) \times 2$$

$$7 + 4 - 6 \qquad\qquad 7 + 1 \times 2$$
$$11 - 6 \qquad\qquad 7 + 2$$
$$5 \qquad\qquad 9$$

$$3 \times (6 + 5) \quad \bigcirc \quad 3 \times 6 + 5$$

$$20 + 80 \div 20 + 5 \quad \bigcirc \quad (20 + 80) \div 20 + 5$$

$$2^2 + (6 \times 3) - 17 \quad \bigcirc \quad 2^2 + 6 \times 3 - 17$$

$$3 \times 20 + 4 \times 2 + 10 \quad \bigcirc \quad 3 \times (20 + 4) \times 2 + 10$$

IXL.com
skill ID
9F5

Let's Learn!

Parentheses aren't the only grouping symbols you can use! You can also use {braces} and [brackets]. To simplify with braces and brackets, work from the inside out.

Try it with $40 \div \{8 \div [(7 - 5) \times 2]\}$.

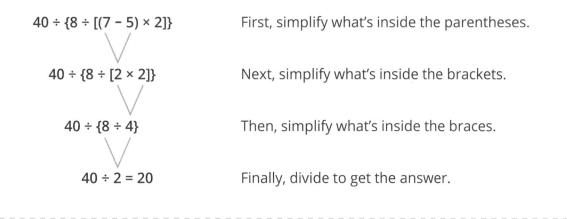

$40 \div \{8 \div [(7 - 5) \times 2]\}$	First, simplify what's inside the parentheses.
$40 \div \{8 \div [2 \times 2]\}$	Next, simplify what's inside the brackets.
$40 \div \{8 \div 4\}$	Then, simplify what's inside the braces.
$40 \div 2 = 20$	Finally, divide to get the answer.

Simplify using the order of operations.

$12 + [25 \div (1 + 4) + 8] = $ _____

$[(24 - 4^2) \times 4] + [10 - (3 \times 2)] = $ _____

$\{6 + [(6 + 3) \times 2]\} \div 3 = $ _____

$\{30 - [(5 + 7) \times (4 \div 2)]\} \div 6 = $ _____

Simplify using the order of operations.

$26 - [10 \div (1 + 1) + 7] =$ _____

$[(6 - 4) \times 3] - [8 - (2 \times 2)] =$ _____

$\{4 + [(1 + 3) \times 9]\} \div 10 =$ _____

$\{3^3 - [(3 + 3) \times (8 \div 4)]\} + 6 =$ _____

$2 \times [(12 + 4) \div (10 - 6) + 8] =$ _____

$[(16 - 12) \times 3] + [5 + (3 \times 2)] =$ _____

$\{9 + [(28 - 5^2) \times 3]\} \div 6 =$ _____

$\{40 - [(3 + 2) \times (12 \div 6)]\} \div 3 =$ _____

Rewrite each story as a numerical expression without solving.

Jeremy had $50 and then spent $10 on a pair of headphones.

$$50 - 10$$

Mitzy's Dance Studio offers 3 tap classes, and each class has 15 spots. The tap teacher then decides to add 1 spot to each of the classes.

$$3 \times (15 + 1)$$

Rachel had 7 plants in her garden. She dug up 3 plants in the morning and planted 5 new ones in the afternoon.

Hannah bought 2 dozen lemon poppyseed muffins from Bower's Bakery. Then she ate 2 of the muffins.

At Camp Willow Tree, the counselors are counting the number of water bottles in the kitchen. They find 3 six-packs and 2 twelve-packs.

Ellie had 2 bags of colorful beads, and each bag had 16 beads. She used 8 beads from each bag to make a necklace.

Match the stories to the numerical expressions. Use each letter once.

A

Each time Kayla volunteers at the animal shelter, she feeds 8 dogs and 4 cats. She feeds the animals twice each visit.

B

There were 8 people on the bus. At the next stop, 2 people got off the bus and 4 people got on.

C

Dayton Library built a display for new books. The display had 2 rows with 3 books on each row. The librarian then added 1 more book to the display.

D

Gilligan sells apples at the farmers' market. He has 2 wagons with 12 bags of apples in each. He also has a display with 5 bags of apples.

E

Tyler picked 12 pumpkins from his family's farm. He kept 2 for himself and divided the remaining ones evenly among 5 friends.

F

Ben wants to triple a cupcake recipe. The batter calls for 2 tablespoons of butter, and the frosting calls for 1 tablespoon of butter.

____D____ 2 × 12 + 5   _____ (12 – 2) ÷ 5

_____ (2 + 1) × 3   _____ (8 + 4) × 2

_____ 8 – 2 + 4   _____ 2 × 3 + 1

Rewrite each story as a numerical expression. Then solve.

Ms. Morrison wants to calculate the number of hours she works each week. She teaches science 6 hours each day, 5 days per week. She also tutors math for 2 hours, twice per week.

$$6 \times 5 + 2 \times 2 = 30 + 4 = 34 \text{ HOURS}$$

Jonathan bought 4 shirts that were $20 each. Then he bought a hat that cost $16 and a pair of shoes that cost $32. He wants to know how much he spent in all.

_____

Mr. Suarez is on a trip to his cousin's house, which is 187 miles away. He has already driven 67 miles. He drives 20 more miles to a gas station and checks the number of miles he has left.

_____

Sydney picked 28 raspberries and 35 blueberries to make two desserts. She needs 4 raspberries for each raspberry tart and 5 blueberries for each blueberry tart. She wants to know how many desserts she will be able to make with the berries.

_____

For more practice, visit IXL.com or the IXL mobile app and enter this code in the search bar.

IXL.com skill ID

Z76

Solve each equation.

$t = 118 - 74$

$t =$ ___44___

$y = 5 \times 12$

$y =$ _____

$m = 56 \div 8$

$m =$ _____

$p = 229 + 142$

$p =$ _____

$r = 100 \div 4$

$r =$ _____

$x = 2 \times 96$

$x =$ _____

$b = 774 \div 18$

$b =$ _____

$q = 1,432 - 859$

$q =$ _____

$a = 38 \times 45$

$a =$ _____

$n = 2,634 + 1,967$

$n =$ _____

$f = 372 \times 23$

$f =$ _____

$w = 1,938 \div 34$

$w =$ _____

Solve each equation. Remember to use the order of operations.

$h = 88 - 12 + 4$

$h =$ _____

$j = 60 \div 30 \times 2$

$j =$ _____

$s = 225 - 100 \div 2$

$s =$ _____

$p = 19 \times 17 + 4$

$p =$ _____

$c = 63 + 13 \times 21$

$c =$ _____

$z = 180 - 126 \div 9$

$z =$ _____

$g = 55 \times 5 + 7 \times 39$

$g =$ _____

$u = 29 + 12 \times 24 - 7$

$u =$ _____

$d = 188 - 14 \times 8 \div 16$

$d =$ _____

IXL.com
skill ID
Z5N

EQUATIONS WITH TWO VARIABLES

Some equations have two variables. For example, $y = x + 5$ has two variables, x and y. If you know the value of one of the variables, then you can solve for the value of the other variable. Look at the examples below.

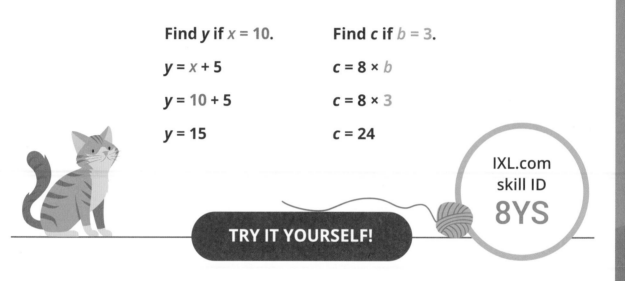

Find y if $x = 10$.

$y = x + 5$

$y = 10 + 5$

$y = 15$

Find c if $b = 3$.

$c = 8 \times b$

$c = 8 \times 3$

$c = 24$

IXL.com
skill ID
8YS

TRY IT YOURSELF!

Solve for the unknown variable.

Find t if $s = 40$.

$t = s - 20$

Find h if $f = 72$.

$h = f \div 9$

Find m if $j = 14$.

$m = j + 6$

Find y if $x = 8$.

$y = 48 \div x$

Write the decimal shown in each model.

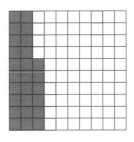

<u>0.26</u>

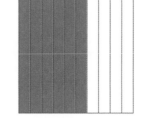

_____

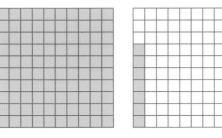

_____

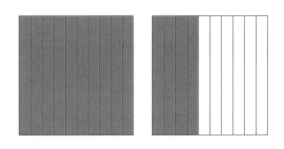

_____

Shade the model to represent each decimal.

0.4

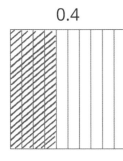

0.37

1.76

2.3

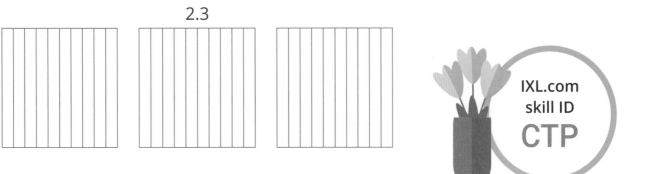

Let's Learn!

Decimal place values are to the right of the decimal point. Look at the place values for the number 836.1427 below.

Hundreds	Tens	Ones	.	Tenths	Hundredths	Thousandths	Ten thousandths
8	3	6	.	1	4	2	7

Circle the digit in the tenths place.

0.⑥5   5.19   8.6   112.83

Circle the digit in the hundredths place.

1.48   62.94   0.582   78.103

Circle the digit in the thousandths place.

5.2941   14.491   6.8278

77.148   12.8481   0.4829

IXL.com
skill ID
X8U

Let's Learn!

The same decimal can be written more than one way. For example, look at the models of 0.8 and 0.80.

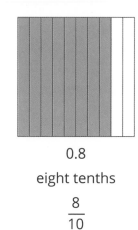

0.8

eight tenths

$\frac{8}{10}$

0.80

eighty hundredths

$\frac{80}{100} = \frac{8}{10}$

The decimals 0.8 and 0.80 are called **equivalent decimals**. That means 0.8 = 0.80! You can make an equivalent decimal by adding zeros to the end or by removing zeros from the end.

Write an equivalent decimal for each number.

0.40 = ____0.4____   6.1 = _____

32.30 = _____   40.99 = _____

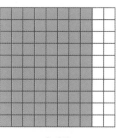

Write two equivalent decimals for each number.

58.700 = ____58.70____ = ____58.7____

3.59 = _____ = _____

0.220 = _____ = _____

IXL.com
skill ID
C2X

Let's Learn!

You can compare decimals by comparing the digits in each place. Try it with 1.47 and 1.44.

1 . 4 7   Compare the whole numbers first. The whole
1 . 4 4   number for both is 1. So, keep going.

1 . 4 7   Compare the tenths place next. The tenths digit
1 . 4 4   for both is 4. So, keep going.

1 . 4 7   Compare the hundredths place next. The 7 is
1 . 4 4   larger than the 4. So, 1.47 > 1.44!

If the decimals have different numbers of digits, you can add zeros to the end of the shorter one. Then keep comparing! To see an example, look at the first problem below.

Compare each pair of decimals using >, <, or =.

5.31 (>) 5.30   4.65 ( ) 4.66   17.1 ( ) 1.71

24.84 ( ) 24.48   25.91 ( ) 26.19   3.10 ( ) 3.1

15.05 ( ) 15.5   29.4 ( ) 2.94   11.1 ( ) 11.01

IXL.com
skill ID
NSG

Write the decimals in order from least to greatest.

2.17   2.08   2.1   <u>2.08</u>   <u>2.1</u>   <u>2.17</u>

46.5   146.5   4.65   _____   _____   _____

303.17   3.71   37.71   _____   _____   _____

2.909   2.991   2.919   _____   _____   _____

6.25   6.524   64.52   6.254   _____   _____   _____   _____

15.818   11.58   15.81   11.5   _____   _____   _____   _____

You can use place value to round decimals. Look one place to the right and round up if that digit is 5 or higher.

Try it yourself! Round to the nearest whole number.

15.43	24.712	11.299	454.3872
15	_____	_____	_____

Round to the nearest tenth.

4.86	211.343	17.06	235.808
4.9	_____	_____	_____

Round to the nearest hundredth.

26.074	88.9013	61.487	221.3913
26.07	_____	_____	_____

Round to the nearest thousandth.

0.4812	2.3871	91.0909	1.00372
0.481	_____	_____	_____

IXL.com
skill ID
MPB

Let's Learn!

When you add decimals, start by lining up the decimal points. Then add! Remember to bring down the decimal point into your answer.

$$\begin{array}{r} 8.41 \\ + 2.23 \\ \hline 10.64 \end{array}$$

Add.

$$\begin{array}{r} {\scriptstyle 1} \\ 4.85 \\ +1.34 \\ \hline 6.19 \end{array}$$

$$\begin{array}{r} 47.6 \\ +13.5 \\ \hline \end{array}$$

$$\begin{array}{r} 62.9 \\ + 8.3 \\ \hline \end{array}$$

$$\begin{array}{r} 29.36 \\ +73.61 \\ \hline \end{array}$$

$$\begin{array}{r} 9.89 \\ +0.57 \\ \hline \end{array}$$

$$\begin{array}{r} 16.71 \\ +24.43 \\ \hline \end{array}$$

$$\begin{array}{r} 93.33 \\ +52.47 \\ \hline \end{array}$$

$$\begin{array}{r} 60.72 \\ +35.41 \\ \hline \end{array}$$

$$\begin{array}{r} 24.61 \\ +77.38 \\ \hline \end{array}$$

$$\begin{array}{r} 120.17 \\ +372.07 \\ \hline \end{array}$$

$$\begin{array}{r} 255.08 \\ + 95.35 \\ \hline \end{array}$$

IXL.com
skill ID
BDX

Add. Remember to line up the decimals first!

13.6 + 5.86 = <u> 19.46 </u>

$$\begin{array}{r} 1 \\ 13.60 \\ + \ 5.86 \\ \hline 19.46 \end{array}$$

29 + 2.64 = _____

19.74 + 8.9 = _____

0.8 + 0.97 = _____

3.1 + 71.42 = _____

17.39 + 5.2 = _____

54.5 + 116.76 = _____

43.68 + 5.7 = _____

86.8 + 4.63 = _____

254.32 + 8.89 = _____

99.85 + 37.2 = _____

84.3 + 63.96 = _____

Let's Learn!

To subtract decimals, first line up the decimal points. Then subtract! Remember to bring down the decimal point into your answer.

$$\begin{array}{r} 19.95 \\ -\ 3.75 \\ \hline 16.20 \end{array}$$

Subtract.

$$\begin{array}{r} {}^{6}\!\!\!\!{}^{10} \\ 2\cancel{7}.\cancel{0}6 \\ -16.94 \\ \hline 10.12 \end{array}$$

$$\begin{array}{r} 3.31 \\ -2.08 \\ \hline \end{array}$$

$$\begin{array}{r} 81.83 \\ -42.32 \\ \hline \end{array}$$

$$\begin{array}{r} 67.12 \\ -29.43 \\ \hline \end{array}$$

$$\begin{array}{r} 8.11 \\ -7.19 \\ \hline \end{array}$$

$$\begin{array}{r} 8.43 \\ -3.67 \\ \hline \end{array}$$

$$\begin{array}{r} 92.59 \\ -\ 7.17 \\ \hline \end{array}$$

$$\begin{array}{r} 49.92 \\ -15.99 \\ \hline \end{array}$$

$$\begin{array}{r} 68.21 \\ -11.59 \\ \hline \end{array}$$

$$\begin{array}{r} 46.14 \\ -\ 8.88 \\ \hline \end{array}$$

$$\begin{array}{r} 153.84 \\ -147.91 \\ \hline \end{array}$$

IXL.com
skill ID
SC8

Subtract. Remember to line up the decimals first!

18.46 − 12.9 = _____5.56_____

24.67 − 15 = _____

```
      7 14
   18.4̶6̶
  −12.90
  ───────
    5.56
```

36.4 − 12.25 = _____

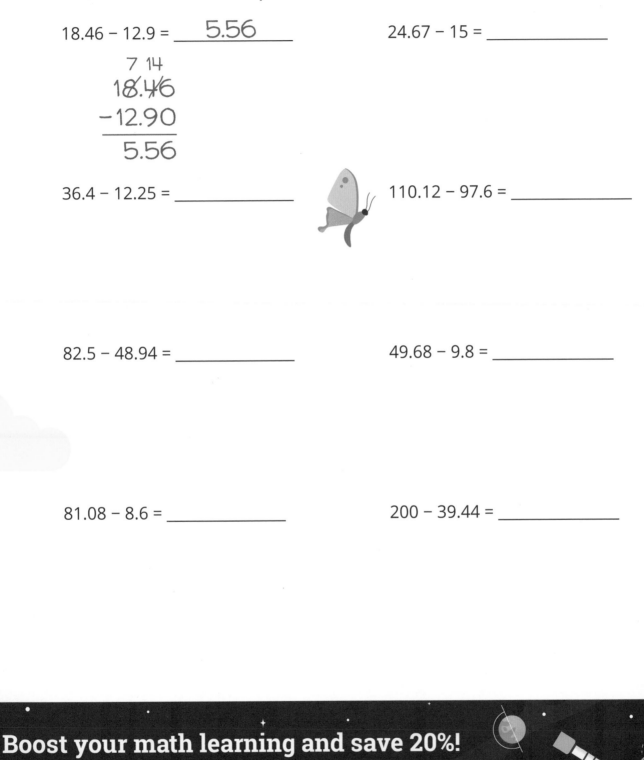

110.12 − 97.6 = _____

82.5 − 48.94 = _____

49.68 − 9.8 = _____

81.08 − 8.6 = _____

200 − 39.44 = _____

Add or subtract.

12.17 − 9.68 = _____

5.8 + 8.35 = _____

9.55 − 8.8 = _____

76.3 − 34.59 = _____

73.5 + 9.96 = _____

6.36 + 13.9 = _____

83 − 20.6 = _____

76.7 + 3.47 = _____

83.13 + 72.8 = _____

130.58 − 7.6 = _____

87.6 + 49.99 = _____

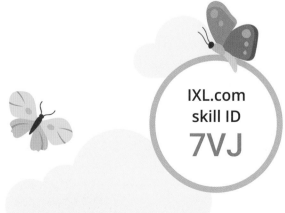

IXL.com
skill ID
7VJ

Use the menu to answer each question.

DINA'S DINER MENU

SALADS

Dina's Delightful Salad........$4.95

Whatcha Taco 'Bout Salad...$5.99

Add chicken, steak, or shrimp to your salad for an extra $2.25.

SANDWICHES

Cheese the Day Burger........$8.80

★ Join the Club Sandwich....$6.25

Best Melt in the Tunaverse..$4.50

★ *Dina's Favorite!*

Jennifer and a few of her friends went to Dina's Diner for lunch. Jennifer ordered Dina's Delightful Salad with chicken. How much did her meal cost?

_____

Colton ordered the Cheese the Day Burger. What is the difference between the price of his meal and the price of Jennifer's meal?

_____

Abby ordered the Join the Club Sandwich. When she paid for her meal, she also included a tip of $1.25. How much did Abby pay?

_____

Evan ordered the Best Melt in the Tunaverse and the Whatcha Taco 'Bout Salad. How much more did his meal cost than Jennifer's meal?

_____

IXL.com
skill ID
35U

Let's Learn!

To multiply a decimal by a whole number, start with the same method as multiplying whole numbers. Try it for 41.27 × 6.

$$
\begin{array}{r}
\overset{1\overset{4}{}}{4\,1\,.\,2\,7} \\
\times 6 \\
\hline
2\,4\,7\,.\,6\,2
\end{array}
$$

Once you've multiplied, you'll need to add a decimal point to the answer.

Count the number of decimal places in the numbers you multiplied. There are two decimal places in 41.27. So, there will be two decimal places in your answer!

So, 41.27 × 6 is 247.62.

Multiply.

$$
\begin{array}{r}
\overset{1}{8}\,.\,3 \\
\times 5 \\
\hline
4\,1\,.\,5
\end{array}
\qquad
\begin{array}{r}
6\,.\,7 \\
\times 8 \\
\hline
\end{array}
\qquad
\begin{array}{r}
1\,6\,.\,4 \\
\times 3 \\
\hline
\end{array}
$$

$$
\begin{array}{r}
2\,.\,5\,9 \\
\times 4 \\
\hline
\end{array}
\qquad
\begin{array}{r}
7\,4\,.\,2\,6 \\
\times 7 \\
\hline
\end{array}
\qquad
\begin{array}{r}
3\,8\,0\,.\,9 \\
\times 9 \\
\hline
\end{array}
$$

IXL.com
skill ID
XNY

Keep going! Multiply.

$$\begin{array}{r} 2.5 \\ \times\ 61 \\ \hline \end{array}$$
$$\begin{array}{r} 8.2 \\ \times\ 19 \\ \hline \end{array}$$
$$\begin{array}{r} 4.6 \\ \times\ 72 \\ \hline \end{array}$$

$$\begin{array}{r} 5.3 \\ \times\ 87 \\ \hline \end{array}$$
$$\begin{array}{r} 3.4 \\ \times\ 58 \\ \hline \end{array}$$
$$\begin{array}{r} 0.49 \\ \times\ 37 \\ \hline \end{array}$$

$$\begin{array}{r} 4.3 \\ \times\ 94 \\ \hline \end{array}$$
$$\begin{array}{r} 0.16 \\ \times\ 52 \\ \hline \end{array}$$
$$\begin{array}{r} 39.3 \\ \times\ 81 \\ \hline \end{array}$$

$$\begin{array}{r} 6.04 \\ \times\ 26 \\ \hline \end{array}$$
$$\begin{array}{r} 72.5 \\ \times\ 98 \\ \hline \end{array}$$
$$\begin{array}{r} 5.69 \\ \times\ 57 \\ \hline \end{array}$$

Multiply.

72.24 × 4 = <u>288.96</u>

$$\begin{array}{r} \overset{1}{72.24} \\ \times \quad\quad 4 \\ \hline 288.96 \end{array}$$

8.214 × 3 = _____

6.8 × 32 = _____

9.3 × 24 = _____

74 × 4.7 = _____

61 × 0.28 = _____

18.6 × 52 = _____

209 × 1.9 = _____

IXL.com
skill ID
PGM

Let's Learn!

When multiplying a decimal by a number like 10, 100, or 1,000, you can move the decimal point to the right based on the number of zeros.

9.432 × 1 = 9.432
9.432 × 10 = 94.32
9.432 × 100 = 943.2
9.432 × 1,000 = 9,432
9.432 × 10,000 = 94,320

Look at the pattern. In the second problem, 10 has one zero. You can move the decimal point one place to the right. Keep moving the decimal point and adding zeros as you go!

Multiply.

16.3 × 1 = _____

16.3 × 10 = _____

16.3 × 100 = _____

16.3 × 1,000 = _____

16.3 × 10,000 = _____

5.05 × 1 = _____

5.05 × 10 = _____

5.05 × 100 = _____

5.05 × 1,000 = _____

5.05 × 10,000 = _____

7.025 × 1 = _____

7.025 × 10 = _____

7.025 × 100 = _____

7.025 × 1,000 = _____

7.025 × 10,000 = _____

65.38 × 1 = _____

65.38 × 10 = _____

65.38 × 100 = _____

65.38 × 1,000 = _____

65.38 × 10,000 = _____

Keep going! Use the pattern to multiply.

$1.94 \times 10 =$ _____

$2.5 \times 100 =$ _____

$6.88 \times 100 =$ _____

$0.99 \times 10 =$ _____

$42.1 \times 1{,}000 =$ _____

$1.36 \times 1{,}000 =$ _____

$5.7 \times 1{,}000 =$ _____

$0.112 \times 100 =$ _____

$2.9 \times 10{,}000 =$ _____

$14.8 \times 1{,}000 =$ _____

$0.2 \times 100{,}000 =$ _____

$9.3 \times 10{,}000 =$ _____

$1.364 \times 1{,}000 =$ _____

$0.17 \times 100{,}000 =$ _____

Exploration Zone

POWERS OF 10

You can rewrite numbers like 10, 100, and 1,000 using exponents, or **powers**. Look at the examples below.

$$10 = 10^1$$
$$100 = 10 \times 10 = 10^2$$
$$1,000 = 10 \times 10 \times 10 = 10^3$$
$$10,000 = 10 \times 10 \times 10 \times 10 = 10^4$$

Powers of 10 can help you multiply decimals quickly. Look at the examples below. Start with the fact that $10^0 = 1$. In each problem, you move the decimal point the same number of spaces as the exponent.

$$3.9 \times 1 = 3.9 \times 10^0 = 3.9$$
$$3.9 \times 10 = 3.9 \times 10^1 = 39.0$$
$$3.9 \times 100 = 3.9 \times 10^2 = 390$$
$$3.9 \times 1,000 = 3.9 \times 10^3 = \underline{\hspace{2cm}}$$
$$3.9 \times 10,000 = 3.9 \times \underline{\hspace{1.5cm}} = \underline{\hspace{2cm}}$$

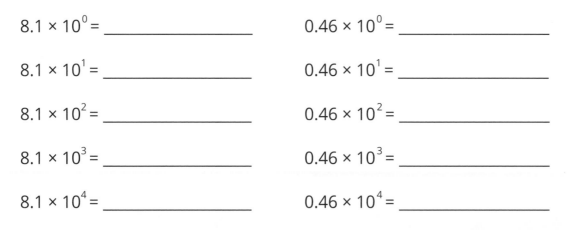

TRY IT YOURSELF!

Use the rule to multiply.

$8.1 \times 10^0 = \underline{\hspace{3cm}}$ $0.46 \times 10^0 = \underline{\hspace{3cm}}$

$8.1 \times 10^1 = \underline{\hspace{3cm}}$ $0.46 \times 10^1 = \underline{\hspace{3cm}}$

$8.1 \times 10^2 = \underline{\hspace{3cm}}$ $0.46 \times 10^2 = \underline{\hspace{3cm}}$

$8.1 \times 10^3 = \underline{\hspace{3cm}}$ $0.46 \times 10^3 = \underline{\hspace{3cm}}$

$8.1 \times 10^4 = \underline{\hspace{3cm}}$ $0.46 \times 10^4 = \underline{\hspace{3cm}}$

Keep going! Use the rule to multiply.

$54.06 \times 10^1 =$ _____

$44.31 \times 10^2 =$ _____

$21.4 \times 10^4 =$ _____

$9.049 \times 10^3 =$ _____

$7.823 \times 10^5 =$ _____

$315.77 \times 10^3 =$ _____

$88.456 \times 10^6 =$ _____

$529.8 \times 10^6 =$ _____

$1.52 \times 10^7 =$ _____

$2.4 \times 10^8 =$ _____

$0.1 \times 10^9 =$ _____

$0.33 \times 10^8 =$ _____

IXL.com
skill ID
92K

Let's Learn!

You can multiply two decimals by following similar steps as before. Try it for 7.6 × 1.9.

$$
\begin{array}{r}
\overset{5}{}7.6 \\
\times\ \ 1.9 \\
\hline
684 \\
+\ 760 \\
\hline
14.44 \\
\end{array}
$$

Look at the numbers you're multiplying. There is one decimal place in 7.6 and one decimal place in 1.9. That means there will be two decimal places in the answer.

So, 7.6 × 1.9 = 14.44!

Multiply.

$$
\begin{array}{r}
\overset{1}{}3.6 \\
\times\ 0.3 \\
\hline
1.08 \\
\end{array}
\qquad
\begin{array}{r}
8.1 \\
\times 0.6 \\
\hline
\end{array}
\qquad
\begin{array}{r}
9.6 \\
\times 0.4 \\
\hline
\end{array}
$$

$$
\begin{array}{r}
2.35 \\
\times\ 0.2 \\
\hline
\end{array}
\qquad
\begin{array}{r}
7.28 \\
\times\ 0.5 \\
\hline
\end{array}
\qquad
\begin{array}{r}
4.75 \\
\times\ 0.8 \\
\hline
\end{array}
$$

IXL.com skill ID

6FA

Multiply.

$$
\begin{array}{r}
5.3 \\
\times\, 2.4 \\
\hline
\end{array}
\qquad
\begin{array}{r}
6.3 \\
\times\, 6.3 \\
\hline
\end{array}
\qquad
\begin{array}{r}
4.5 \\
\times\, 2.1 \\
\hline
\end{array}
$$

$$
\begin{array}{r}
9.7 \\
\times\, 8.6 \\
\hline
\end{array}
\qquad
\begin{array}{r}
0.64 \\
\times\ \ 3.7 \\
\hline
\end{array}
\qquad
\begin{array}{r}
9.9 \\
\times\, 9.9 \\
\hline
\end{array}
$$

$$
\begin{array}{r}
3.02 \\
\times\ \ 1.4 \\
\hline
\end{array}
\qquad
\begin{array}{r}
5.96 \\
\times\ \ 2.2 \\
\hline
\end{array}
\qquad
\begin{array}{r}
2.88 \\
\times\ \ 4.6 \\
\hline
\end{array}
$$

$$
\begin{array}{r}
8.24 \\
\times\ \ 1.7 \\
\hline
\end{array}
\qquad
\begin{array}{r}
7.65 \\
\times\ \ 3.3 \\
\hline
\end{array}
\qquad
\begin{array}{r}
9.89 \\
\times\ \ 5.8 \\
\hline
\end{array}
$$

IXL.com
skill ID
FLL

Multiply.

9.75 × 0.3 = _____

0.5 × 19.2 = _____

46.4 × 0.4 = _____

3.2 × 1.8 = _____

1.5 × 6.4 = _____

8.8 × 7.9 = _____

3.08 × 0.32 = _____

0.25 × 38.4 = _____

TAKE ANOTHER LOOK!

There are three problems on this page that have equivalent answers. Can you find them?

Answer each question.

Ava wants to buy 2 books at the bookstore. Each book costs $14.95. How much money does she need to buy both books?

_____

Ellen's baby sister is 23.5 inches tall. Ellen is 2.5 times as tall as her baby sister. How many inches tall is Ellen?

_____

Gavin bought 0.75 pounds of Swiss cheese at the grocery store. The cheese was on sale for $4.60 per pound. How much did Gavin pay?

_____

Julia has 3 bird feeders that each hold 3.4 pounds of birdseed. She also has 2 bird feeders that each hold 5.1 pounds of birdseed. How many pounds of birdseed does she need to fill all of her bird feeders?

_____

Landon is training for a race called a triathlon. In the triathlon, he will need to swim, bike, and run. Answer each question about his race.

In the race, Landon must bike for 6.2 miles. Then he will run about 0.25 times as many miles as he bikes. About how far will Landon run in the triathlon?

_____

Landon will also swim 0.25 miles in the race. He swam this distance at 9 training sessions last month. What is the total distance Landon swam in all his training sessions last month?

_____

In his first month of training, Landon biked 3.1 miles and ran 0.75 miles each workout. He completed 18 workouts that month. What is the total distance that he ran and biked in his first month of training?

_____

Landon biked 6.2 miles on Saturday to prepare for his race. On Sunday, he biked 0.5 times as many miles as Saturday. What total distance did he bike on Saturday and Sunday?

_____

IXL.com
skill ID
83A

Let's Learn!

You can use long division to divide a decimal by a whole number. Try it with 9.6 ÷ 4.

```
     2.4
  4 ) 9.6
     -8
      1 6
     -1 6
        0
```

Divide the way you would for 96 ÷ 4, but remember to include a decimal point in your answer. The decimal point will go above the decimal point in the dividend.

So, 9.6 ÷ 4 = 2.4.

Divide.

```
     4.5
  3 ) 13.5
     -12
      15
     -15
       0
```

6) 95.4

4) 1.28

9) 218.7

11) 41.8

14) 869.4

Let's Learn!

Sometimes you have to add on zeros to the end of the dividend to keep dividing. Try it with 8.7 ÷ 2.

```
     4.35
  2 ) 8.70
    −8
     0 7
       6
      10
   −  10
       0
```

Follow the same steps for division as before.

Instead of writing your answer with a remainder, add on a zero and keep dividing! Remember that 8.7 is the same as 8.70.

So, 8.7 ÷ 2 is 4.35!

Divide.

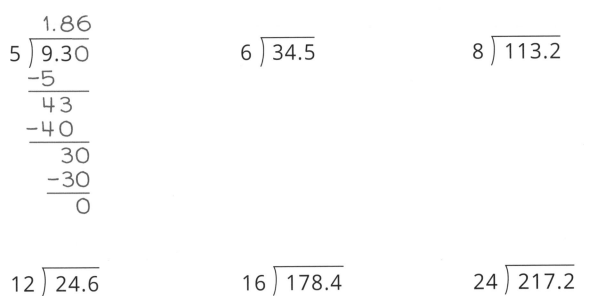

```
     1.86
  5 ) 9.30
    −5
     43
    −40
      30
     −30
       0
```

```
  6 ) 34.5
```

```
  8 ) 113.2
```

```
  12 ) 24.6
```

```
  16 ) 178.4
```

```
  24 ) 217.2
```

Divide.

$9\overline{)11.61}$ $\qquad$ $8\overline{)72.4}$ $\qquad$ $11\overline{)81.4}$

$16\overline{)76.96}$ $\qquad$ $21\overline{)115.5}$ $\qquad$ $15\overline{)48.3}$

$12\overline{)61.8}$ $\qquad$ $14\overline{)46.06}$ $\qquad$ $25\overline{)200.5}$

$22\overline{)74.36}$ $\qquad$ $36\overline{)223.2}$

IXL.com
skill ID
NLL

Let's Learn!

When you divide by powers of 10, you can move the decimal point to the left based on the number of zeros. Try it with 15.2. See the pattern below!

15.2 ÷ 1 = 15.2
15.2 ÷ 10 = 1.52
15.2 ÷ 100 = 0.152
15.2 ÷ 1,000 = 0.0152
15.2 ÷ 10,000 = 0.00152

Divide.

7.4 ÷ 1 = _____

7.4 ÷ 10 = _____

7.4 ÷ 100 = _____

7.4 ÷ 1,000 = _____

7.4 ÷ 10,000 = _____

33.89 ÷ 1 = _____

33.89 ÷ 10 = _____

33.89 ÷ 100 = _____

33.89 ÷ 1,000 = _____

33.89 ÷ 10,000 = _____

2.53 ÷ 1 = _____

2.53 ÷ 10 = _____

2.53 ÷ 100 = _____

2.53 ÷ 1,000 = _____

2.53 ÷ 10,000 = _____

0.9 ÷ 1 = _____

0.9 ÷ 10 = _____

0.9 ÷ 100 = _____

0.9 ÷ 1,000 = _____

0.9 ÷ 10,000 = _____

Keep going! Use the pattern to divide.

8.6 ÷ 10 = _____

5.14 ÷ 100 = _____

445.1 ÷ 100 = _____

52.3 ÷ 1,000 = _____

8 ÷ 100 = _____

9.2 ÷ 1,000 = _____

0.76 ÷ 100 = _____

52.7 ÷ 10,000 = _____

1.28 ÷ 1,000 = _____

3 ÷ 10,000 = _____

0.4 ÷ 100,000 = _____

1.7 ÷ 100,000 = _____

| **THINK ABOUT IT!** | Using what you know about powers of 10, can you use the same method to solve $1.7 \div 10^6$? What about $1.7 \div 10^7$? |

Let's Learn!

You can use long division to divide a decimal by a decimal, too.
Try it with 12.32 ÷ 0.8.

$$0.8 \overline{)12.32}$$

Start by changing the divisor to a whole number. You can do that by multiplying by 10, since 12.32 ÷ 0.8 is the same as 123.2 ÷ 8. Change 0.8 to 8, and change 12.32 to 123.2.

```
        15.4
  8 ) 123.2
    − 8
      43
    − 40
      32
    − 32
        0
```

Notice that for both numbers, you've moved the decimal point one place to the right.

Use long division to divide the decimal 123.2 by the whole number 8.

So, 12.32 ÷ 0.8 = 15.4.

Divide.

```
          14.7
  0.6 ) 8.82
      −6
       28
      −24
       42
      −42
        0
```

$$0.4 \overline{)4.48}$$

$$0.7 \overline{)12.81}$$

$$1.1 \overline{)3.85}$$

$$1.2 \overline{)29.52}$$

$$1.7 \overline{)43.86}$$

Divide.

$1.9 \overline{)9.31}$ 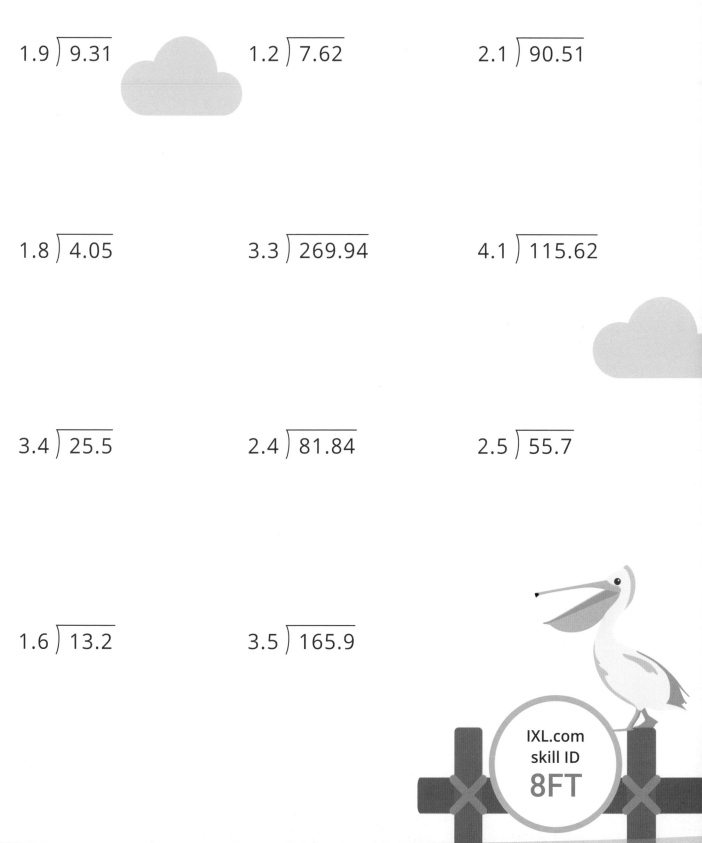 $\qquad$ $1.2 \overline{)7.62}$ $\qquad$ $2.1 \overline{)90.51}$

$1.8 \overline{)4.05}$ $\qquad$ $3.3 \overline{)269.94}$ $\qquad$ $4.1 \overline{)115.62}$

$3.4 \overline{)25.5}$ $\qquad$ $2.4 \overline{)81.84}$ $\qquad$ $2.5 \overline{)55.7}$

$1.6 \overline{)13.2}$ $\qquad$ $3.5 \overline{)165.9}$

Solve each set of division problems. Then write your answers in the puzzle below. Your answers will share a decimal point.

5.67 ÷ 0.3 = __18.9__

40.6 ÷ 14 = __2.9__

68.4 ÷ 9 = _____

7.08 ÷ 0.8 = _____

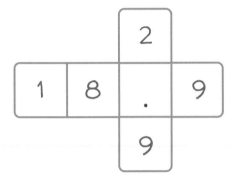

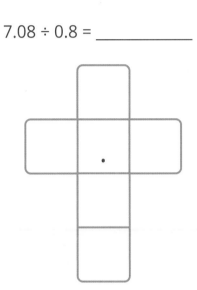

153.45 ÷ 33 = _____

32.24 ÷ 2.6 = _____

97.56 ÷ 18 = _____

16.32 ÷ 1.7 = _____

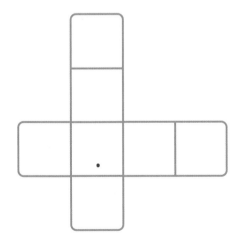

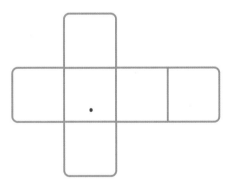

Answer each question.

Justin is building a brick path in his garden. The path is 4 bricks wide, and the total width of the path is 14.6 inches. If each brick is the same size, what is the width of each brick?

_____

Last year, Oliver took 3 trips to visit his cousin. He traveled a total of 206.7 miles for all the trips. How far did he travel on each trip?

_____

Cassidy and 5 of her friends earned a total of $275.40 selling homemade jewelry at the Holiday Craft Market. If they divide the money evenly, how much will each person get?

_____

Aaron buys 1.6 pounds of green beans for $3.92. He buys 2.1 pounds of asparagus for $6.09. Which vegetable is cheaper per pound?

_____

Exploration Zone

DECIMAL QUOTIENTS

When two whole numbers don't divide evenly, you can write the answer using a decimal! For example, find 186 ÷ 8.

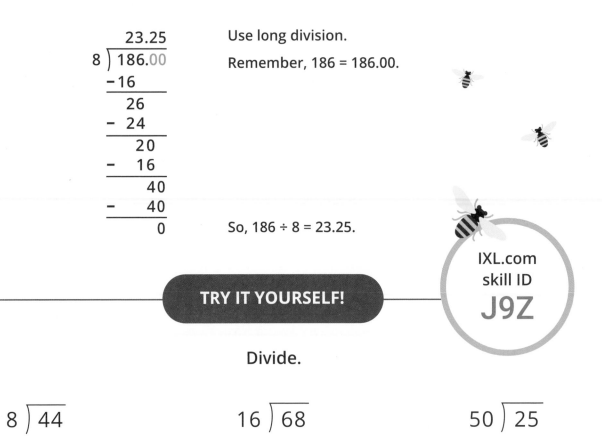

```
        23.25
   8 ) 186.00
      −16
        26
      − 24
        20
      −  16
         40
      −  40
          0
```

Use long division.

Remember, 186 = 186.00.

So, 186 ÷ 8 = 23.25.

TRY IT YOURSELF!

IXL.com
skill ID
J9Z

Divide.

$8 \overline{)44}$ $16 \overline{)68}$ $50 \overline{)25}$

Answer each question. Write your answer using a decimal.

Addison had 20 ounces of cashews, and she split the cashews equally between 8 different salads. How many ounces of cashews were in each salad?

_____

Matthew and 7 of his friends went miniature golfing. The total cost was $70, and they split the cost evenly. How much did each person pay?

_____

Jackie bought a 2-pound bag of lemons. There were 10 lemons in the bag. If all the lemons were about the same size, about how much did each one weigh?

_____

Sensational Slime Lab divides 18 ounces of slime into 24 small jars. Each jar contains the same amount of slime. How many ounces are in each jar?

_____

IXL.com
skill ID
Z2X

Write the fraction shown.

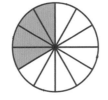

$\dfrac{1}{6}$ _____

_____

_____

Answer each question.

What fraction of the animals are birds?	What fraction of the slices have jam?	What fraction of the items are rackets?

_____

_____

_____

Write the fraction shown.

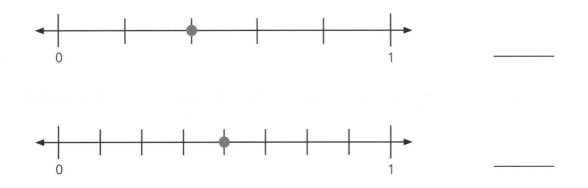

_____

_____

Shade in each fraction.

$$\frac{3}{9}$$

$$\frac{7}{8}$$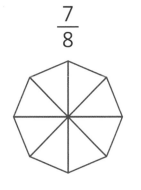

$$\frac{2}{3}$$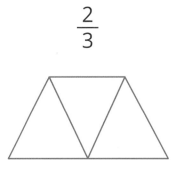

Shade in each fraction.

$$\frac{1}{5}$$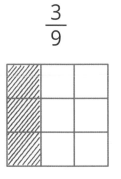

$$\frac{5}{9}$$

$$\frac{4}{11}$$

Show each fraction on the number line.

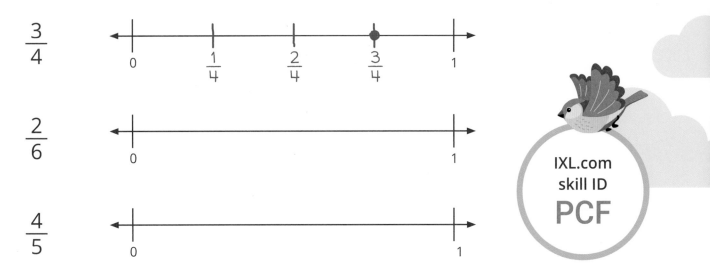

$$\frac{3}{4}$$

$$\frac{2}{6}$$

$$\frac{4}{5}$$

To make an equivalent fraction, multiply or divide the numerator and denominator by the same number. Try it yourself! Write an equivalent fraction for each of the following fractions.

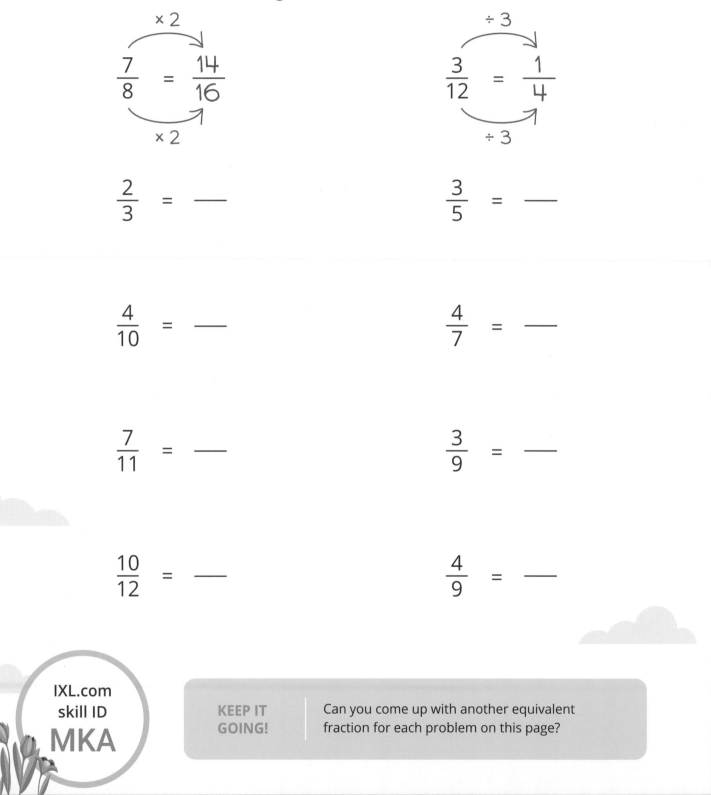

$$\frac{7}{8} = \frac{14}{16}$$
$$\times 2 \qquad \times 2$$

$$\frac{3}{12} = \frac{1}{4}$$
$$\div 3 \qquad \div 3$$

$$\frac{2}{3} = —$$

$$\frac{3}{5} = —$$

$$\frac{4}{10} = —$$

$$\frac{4}{7} = —$$

$$\frac{7}{11} = —$$

$$\frac{3}{9} = —$$

$$\frac{10}{12} = —$$

$$\frac{4}{9} = —$$

KEEP IT GOING! Can you come up with another equivalent fraction for each problem on this page?

Let's Learn!

You can write a fraction in **simplest form** by dividing the numerator and denominator by their **greatest common factor (GCF)**.

Let's try it for $\frac{8}{12}$. To find the GCF, write out the factors of each number. Look at the factors they share, and circle the largest one. The GCF of 8 and 12 is 4.

Factors of 8: 1, 2, ④, 8

Factors of 12: 1, 2, 3, ④, 6, 12

To get the simplest form of $\frac{8}{12}$, divide the numerator and denominator by the GCF, 4.

So, the simplest form of $\frac{8}{12}$ is $\frac{2}{3}$.

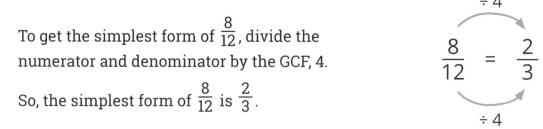

$$\div 4$$
$$\frac{8}{12} = \frac{2}{3}$$
$$\div 4$$

Find the GCF. Then divide to write each fraction in simplest form.

Factors of 2: _____

Factors of 6: _____

$$\frac{2}{6} = \underline{\quad}$$

Factors of 4: _____

Factors of 16: _____

$$\frac{4}{16} = \underline{\quad}$$

Factors of 10: _____

Factors of 15: _____

$$\frac{10}{15} = \underline{\quad}$$

IXL.com
skill ID
4C2

Write each fraction in simplest form.

$$\frac{5}{35} = \underline{\quad}$$ $$\frac{14}{20} = \underline{\quad}$$ $$\frac{22}{24} = \underline{\quad}$$

$$\frac{8}{64} = \underline{\quad}$$ $$\frac{11}{55} = \underline{\quad}$$ $$\frac{5}{60} = \underline{\quad}$$

$$\frac{16}{24} = \underline{\quad}$$ $$\frac{12}{48} = \underline{\quad}$$ $$\frac{27}{63} = \underline{\quad}$$

$$\frac{25}{45} = \underline{\quad}$$ $$\frac{36}{40} = \underline{\quad}$$ $$\frac{18}{30} = \underline{\quad}$$

$$\frac{24}{60} = \underline{\quad}$$ $$\frac{15}{33} = \underline{\quad}$$ $$\frac{20}{35} = \underline{\quad}$$

$$\frac{10}{100} = \underline{\quad}$$ $$\frac{45}{63} = \underline{\quad}$$

IXL.com
skill ID
A76

Let's Learn!

You can write a fraction as a decimal, since they both represent parts of a whole. First, find an equivalent fraction that has a denominator of 10 or 100. Then, write the decimal using place value. Try it for $\frac{3}{4}$.

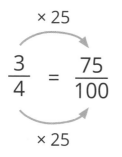

$$\frac{3}{4} = \frac{75}{100}$$

× 25

× 25

Place value chart			
Ones		Tenths	Hundredths
0	.	7	5

Write each fraction as a decimal.

Fraction	Equivalent fraction	Decimal
$\frac{1}{5}$	$\frac{2}{10}$	0.2
$\frac{41}{50}$		
$\frac{11}{20}$		
$\frac{1}{2}$		
$\frac{27}{50}$		
$\frac{17}{25}$		

IXL.com skill ID

6QG

Keep going! Write each fraction as a decimal.

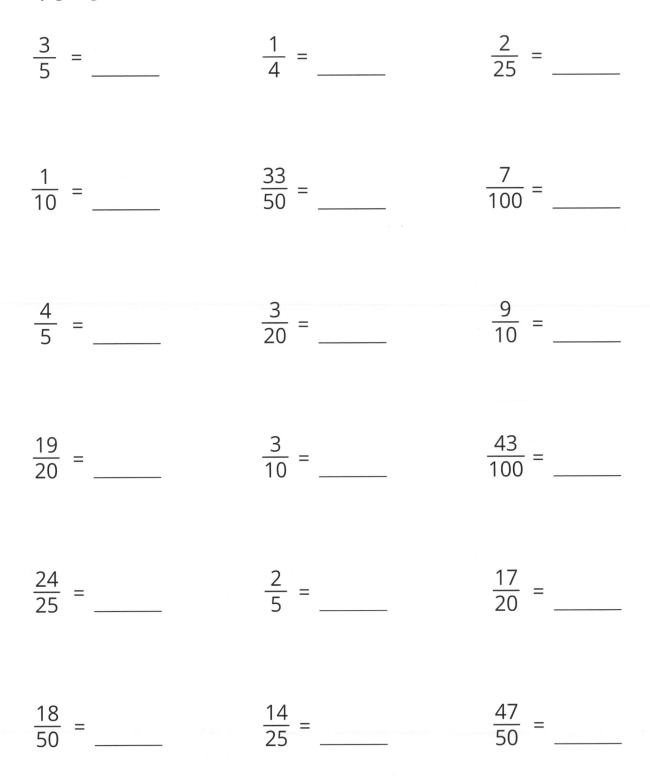

$\dfrac{3}{5}$ = _____

$\dfrac{1}{4}$ = _____

$\dfrac{2}{25}$ = _____

$\dfrac{1}{10}$ = _____

$\dfrac{33}{50}$ = _____

$\dfrac{7}{100}$ = _____

$\dfrac{4}{5}$ = _____

$\dfrac{3}{20}$ = _____

$\dfrac{9}{10}$ = _____

$\dfrac{19}{20}$ = _____

$\dfrac{3}{10}$ = _____

$\dfrac{43}{100}$ = _____

$\dfrac{24}{25}$ = _____

$\dfrac{2}{5}$ = _____

$\dfrac{17}{20}$ = _____

$\dfrac{18}{50}$ = _____

$\dfrac{14}{25}$ = _____

$\dfrac{47}{50}$ = _____

Let's Learn!

You can go the other direction, too! To write a decimal as a fraction, use place value to find the denominator. Try it for 0.7.

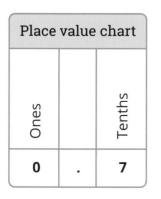

Place value chart		
Ones		Tenths
0	.	7

Your fraction will have a denominator of 10, since 0.7 is the same as seven tenths.

$$0.7 = \frac{7}{10}$$

Write each decimal as a fraction in simplest form.

0.87 = $\dfrac{87}{100}$

0.6 = $\dfrac{6}{10} = \dfrac{3}{5}$

0.8 = _____

0.51 = _____

0.9 = _____

0.75 = _____

0.16 = _____

0.01 = _____

0.2 = _____

0.58 = _____

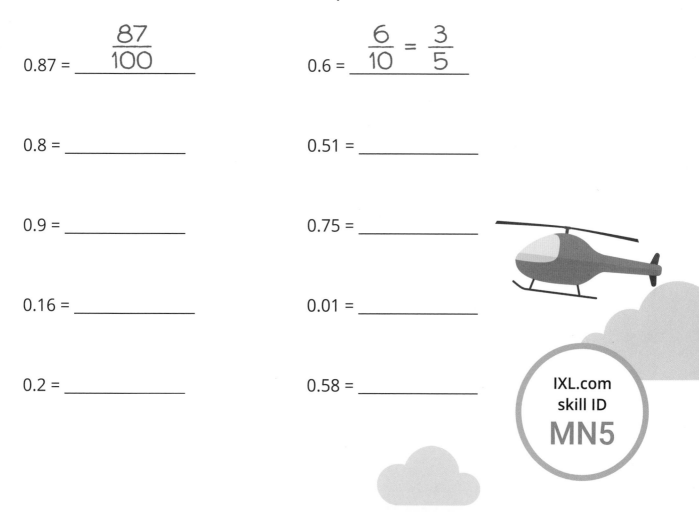

IXL.com
skill ID
MN5

Compare each pair using >, <, or =.

0.5 $\boxed{<}$ $\frac{3}{4}$ 0.23 $\bigcirc$ $\frac{1}{5}$ $\frac{90}{100}$ $\bigcirc$ 0.29

0.63 $\bigcirc$ $\frac{1}{2}$ $\frac{7}{10}$ $\bigcirc$ 0.8   0.81 $\bigcirc$ $\frac{8}{10}$

$\frac{1}{4}$ $\bigcirc$ 0.19   0.55 $\bigcirc$ $\frac{6}{10}$ $\frac{1}{25}$ $\bigcirc$ 0.04

$\frac{25}{50}$ $\bigcirc$ 0.25   0.4 $\bigcirc$ $\frac{8}{20}$ $\frac{16}{20}$ $\bigcirc$ 0.85

$\frac{3}{5}$ $\bigcirc$ 0.6 $\frac{3}{100}$ $\bigcirc$ 0.3   0.95 $\bigcirc$ $\frac{24}{25}$

Let's Learn!

Fractions and decimals are related to **percents**. A percent is 1 part out of 100, and it is written with the % sign.

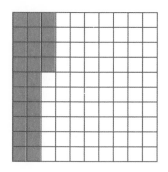

If you have 24%, you have 24 parts out of 100. That is the same as $\frac{24}{100}$ or 0.24. This model shows 0.24, which is the same as 24%.

Write the percent shown in the model.

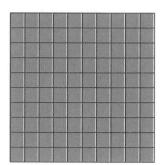

_____

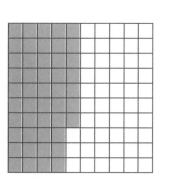

_____

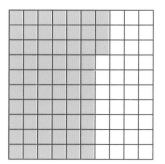

_____

_____

_____

Let's Learn!

You can change a percent to a decimal. Try it with 9%. Since a percent is out of 100, you can write 9% as 9 out of 100, or $\frac{9}{100}$. That is the same as nine hundredths, or 0.09.

$$9\% = 0.09$$

As a rule, you can change a percent to a decimal by moving the decimal point 2 places to the left.

Write each percent as a decimal.

26% = <u>0.26</u>   12% = _____   5% = _____   40% = _____

1% = _____   76% = _____   22% = _____   100% = _____

89% = _____   20% = _____   17% = _____   71% = _____

93% = _____   35% = _____   49% = _____   6% = _____

You can go the other direction, too! Write each decimal as a percent.

0.9 = __90%__   0.04 = _____   0.23 = _____   0.6 = _____

0.91 = _____   0.77 = _____   0.01 = _____   0.84 = _____

1.00 = _____   0.5 = _____   0.73 = _____   0.16 = _____

0.65 = _____   0.81 = _____   0.29 = _____   0.3 = _____

FRACTIONS AND PERCENTS

You can rewrite fractions as percents, too! Use what you know about fractions and decimals to help. Try it with $\frac{4}{5}$.

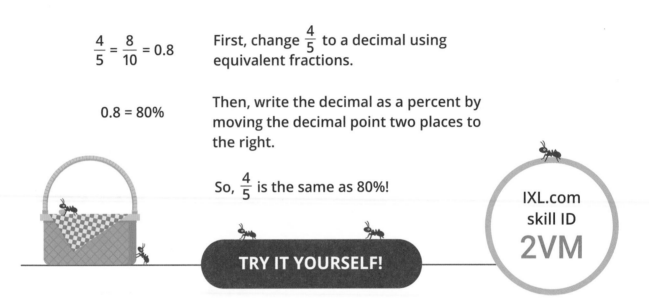

$\frac{4}{5} = \frac{8}{10} = 0.8$ First, change $\frac{4}{5}$ to a decimal using equivalent fractions.

$0.8 = 80\%$ Then, write the decimal as a percent by moving the decimal point two places to the right.

So, $\frac{4}{5}$ is the same as 80%!

TRY IT YOURSELF!

IXL.com
skill ID
2VM

Answer each question.

In the spring parade, $\frac{3}{4}$ of the floats were decorated with flowers. What percentage of the floats were decorated with flowers?   _____

Megan answered $\frac{17}{20}$ of the questions correctly in a game of trivia. What percentage of the trivia questions did she answer correctly?   _____

Keep going! Answer each question.

A chemistry teacher filled a test tube $\frac{1}{2}$ full with a chemical solution. What percentage of the test tube was filled with the chemical solution?

_____

Members of a travel club are planning a trip to Europe, and $\frac{1}{5}$ of them have never been. What percentage of the members in the group have never been to Europe?

_____

A book publisher surveyed its customers to see whether they preferred paperback books, audiobooks, or ebooks. In the survey, $\frac{3}{10}$ of the customers chose audiobooks. What percentage of the customers chose audiobooks?

_____

The audience for the Fancy Feet Ice Skating Show filled $\frac{43}{50}$ of the seats in the ice rink. What percentage of the seats were filled?

_____

Let's Learn!

You can add and subtract fractions. If the fractions have like denominators, just add or subtract the numerators. The denominators will stay the same.

$$\frac{1}{5} + \frac{3}{5} = \frac{4}{5} \qquad \frac{3}{7} - \frac{2}{7} = \frac{1}{7}$$

Add or subtract. Write your answer in simplest form.

$$\frac{5}{9} + \frac{1}{9} = \frac{6}{9} = \frac{2}{3}$$

$$\frac{7}{8} - \frac{3}{8} = \underline{\hspace{2cm}}$$

$$\frac{9}{10} - \frac{3}{10} = \underline{\hspace{2cm}}$$

$$\frac{1}{3} + \frac{1}{3} = \underline{\hspace{2cm}}$$

$$\frac{4}{11} + \frac{6}{11} = \underline{\hspace{2cm}}$$

$$\frac{11}{12} - \frac{7}{12} = \underline{\hspace{2cm}}$$

$$\frac{6}{7} - \frac{5}{7} = \underline{\hspace{2cm}}$$

$$\frac{14}{15} - \frac{11}{15} = \underline{\hspace{2cm}}$$

$$\frac{3}{16} + \frac{3}{16} = \underline{\hspace{2cm}}$$

$$\frac{13}{14} - \frac{1}{14} = \underline{\hspace{2cm}}$$

$$\frac{7}{12} - \frac{1}{12} = \underline{\hspace{2cm}}$$

IXL.com
skill ID
FXW

Let's Learn!

To add fractions with different denominators, you can make equivalent fractions using the **least common denominator (LCD)**. The LCD is the smallest common multiple of both denominators.
Try it for $\frac{1}{4} + \frac{3}{5}$.

To find the LCD, write a few multiples of each denominator. Circle the smallest multiple they share. Here, the LCD is 20.

Multiples of 4: 4, 8, 12, 16, ⓩⓞ
Multiples of 5: 5, 10, 15, ⓩⓞ

Make equivalent fractions using the LCD as the denominator, and then add.

$$\frac{1}{4} + \frac{3}{5}$$
$$\downarrow \qquad \downarrow$$
$$\frac{5}{20} + \frac{12}{20} = \frac{17}{20}$$

Add. Write your answer in simplest form.

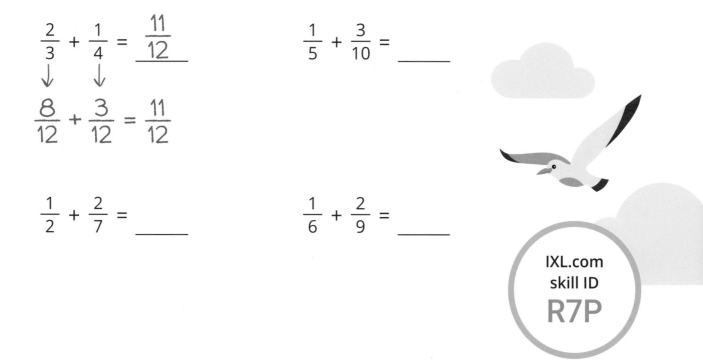

$$\frac{2}{3} + \frac{1}{4} = \frac{11}{12}$$
$$\downarrow \qquad \downarrow$$
$$\frac{8}{12} + \frac{3}{12} = \frac{11}{12}$$

$$\frac{1}{5} + \frac{3}{10} = \underline{\qquad}$$

$$\frac{1}{2} + \frac{2}{7} = \underline{\qquad}$$

$$\frac{1}{6} + \frac{2}{9} = \underline{\qquad}$$

IXL.com
skill ID
R7P

Keep going! Add. Write your answer in simplest form.

$\dfrac{1}{4} + \dfrac{1}{6} = \dfrac{3}{12} + \dfrac{2}{12} = \dfrac{5}{12}$ _____

$\dfrac{1}{2} + \dfrac{2}{9} =$ _____

$\dfrac{3}{8} + \dfrac{1}{6} =$ _____

$\dfrac{3}{4} + \dfrac{1}{12} =$ _____

$\dfrac{1}{10} + \dfrac{1}{4} =$ _____

$\dfrac{2}{3} + \dfrac{1}{8} =$ _____

$\dfrac{1}{3} + \dfrac{2}{5} =$ _____

$\dfrac{3}{5} + \dfrac{2}{7} =$ _____

$\dfrac{5}{12} + \dfrac{3}{8} =$ _____

$\dfrac{2}{11} + \dfrac{3}{4} =$ _____

Let's Learn!

To subtract fractions with different denominators, make equivalent fractions using the LCD. Then subtract. Try it for $\frac{5}{7} - \frac{1}{2}$.

$$\frac{5}{7} - \frac{1}{2}$$

$$\frac{10}{14} - \frac{7}{14} = \frac{3}{14}$$

Subtract. Write your answer in simplest form.

$\frac{4}{5} - \frac{2}{3} = \dfrac{12}{15} - \dfrac{10}{15} = \dfrac{2}{15}$ $\frac{3}{4} - \frac{1}{2} = $ _____

$\frac{11}{12} - \frac{5}{6} = $ _____ $\frac{3}{5} - \frac{1}{4} = $ _____

$\frac{6}{7} - \frac{1}{3} = $ _____ $\frac{9}{10} - \frac{2}{5} = $ _____

$\frac{5}{6} - \frac{3}{8} = $ _____ $\frac{3}{4} - \frac{3}{7} = $ _____

Add or subtract. Write your answer in simplest form.

$\dfrac{1}{5} + \dfrac{3}{7} =$ _____

$\dfrac{4}{5} - \dfrac{1}{4} =$ _____

$\dfrac{1}{9} + \dfrac{2}{3} =$ _____

$\dfrac{8}{11} - \dfrac{1}{2} =$ _____

$\dfrac{5}{6} - \dfrac{4}{7} =$ _____

$\dfrac{1}{10} + \dfrac{2}{5} =$ _____

$\dfrac{3}{8} + \dfrac{1}{3} =$ _____

$\dfrac{8}{9} - \dfrac{3}{4} =$ _____

$\dfrac{5}{6} - \dfrac{1}{8} =$ _____

$\dfrac{3}{10} + \dfrac{7}{12} =$ _____

IXL.com
skill ID
FCA

Add or subtract to follow the path. Write each fraction in simplest form.

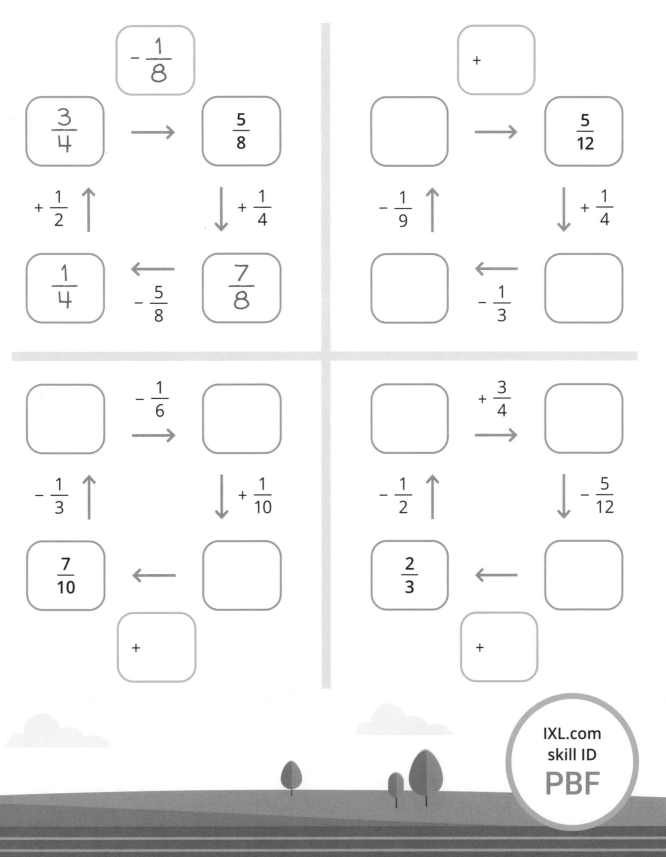

Answer each question. Write your answer in simplest form.

Emery is making the filling for an apple pie. She combines $\frac{3}{4}$ of a teaspoon of cinnamon and $\frac{1}{8}$ of a teaspoon of nutmeg in a bowl. How many teaspoons of spice are in the bowl?

_____

The owners of Alpine Ski Shop decide to have a sale on ski hats. Their goal is to sell $\frac{2}{3}$ of their ski hats. They have sold $\frac{3}{7}$ of their ski hats so far. What fraction do they still need to sell?

_____

Gina uses 2 equal-size jars to store dry oatmeal. The first jar is $\frac{1}{5}$ full, and the second jar is $\frac{1}{2}$ full. To save space in her pantry, she pours all of the oatmeal into the second jar. How full is the second jar now?

_____

Ryan mixes $\frac{3}{4}$ of a gallon of white paint with $\frac{1}{6}$ of a gallon of blue paint. He then uses $\frac{5}{6}$ of a gallon of the paint. How much does he have left?

_____

IXL.com
skill ID
TCD

Write each amount as a mixed number and an improper fraction.

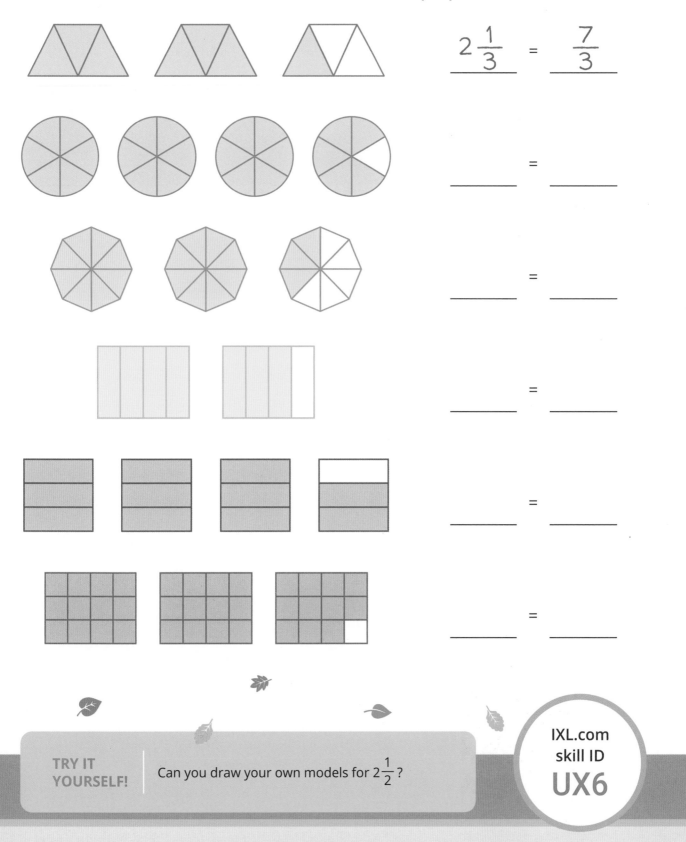

$2\dfrac{1}{3}$ = $\dfrac{7}{3}$

_____ = _____

_____ = _____

_____ = _____

_____ = _____

_____ = _____

TRY IT YOURSELF! | Can you draw your own models for $2\dfrac{1}{2}$?

Write the mixed numbers as improper fractions.

$2\dfrac{1}{6} = \dfrac{13}{6}$

$1\dfrac{2}{3} = \rule{2cm}{0.4pt}$

$2\dfrac{3}{5} = \rule{2cm}{0.4pt}$

$1\dfrac{1}{9} = \rule{2cm}{0.4pt}$

$3\dfrac{3}{4} = \rule{2cm}{0.4pt}$

$2\dfrac{4}{7} = \rule{2cm}{0.4pt}$

$1\dfrac{9}{10} = \rule{2cm}{0.4pt}$

$2\dfrac{5}{6} = \rule{2cm}{0.4pt}$

$3\dfrac{2}{9} = \rule{2cm}{0.4pt}$

$2\dfrac{7}{8} = \rule{2cm}{0.4pt}$

$3\dfrac{5}{12} = \rule{2cm}{0.4pt}$

$3\dfrac{10}{11} = \rule{2cm}{0.4pt}$

UNLOCK THE SECRET! Can you come up with a rule for converting mixed numbers to improper fractions?

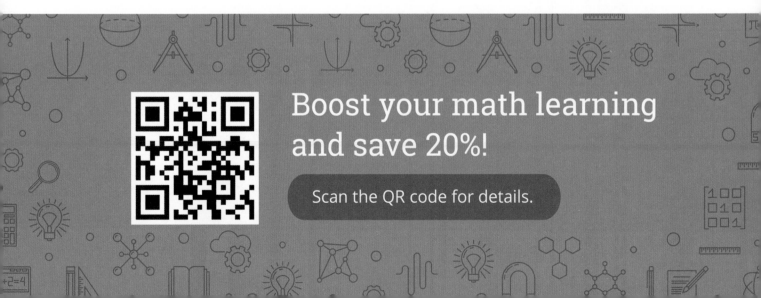

Write the improper fractions as mixed numbers in simplest form.

$\frac{10}{8}$ = $1\frac{2}{8} = 1\frac{1}{4}$

$\frac{9}{4}$ = _____

$\frac{13}{7}$ = _____

$\frac{9}{6}$ = _____

$\frac{14}{4}$ = _____

$\frac{13}{5}$ = _____

$\frac{35}{10}$ = _____

$\frac{31}{11}$ = _____

$\frac{25}{7}$ = _____

$\frac{46}{12}$ = _____

$\frac{24}{9}$ = _____

FIND THE RULE! | Can you come up with a rule for converting improper fractions to mixed numbers?

IXL.com
skill ID
B7X

Let's Learn!

You can add mixed numbers by adding the whole numbers and then adding the fractions. Try it with $3\frac{1}{4} + 2\frac{5}{8}$.

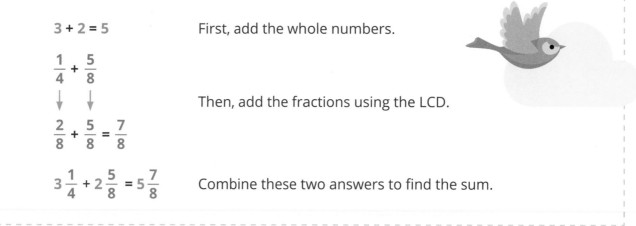

$3 + 2 = 5$ First, add the whole numbers.

$\frac{1}{4} + \frac{5}{8}$

$\downarrow \quad \downarrow$

$\frac{2}{8} + \frac{5}{8} = \frac{7}{8}$ Then, add the fractions using the LCD.

$3\frac{1}{4} + 2\frac{5}{8} = 5\frac{7}{8}$ Combine these two answers to find the sum.

Add. Write your answer as a mixed number in simplest form.

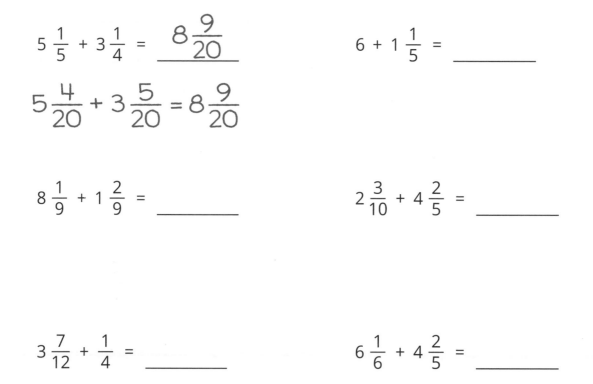

$5\frac{1}{5} + 3\frac{1}{4} = \underline{\ 8\frac{9}{20}\ }$

$6 + 1\frac{1}{5} = \underline{\qquad}$

$5\frac{4}{20} + 3\frac{5}{20} = 8\frac{9}{20}$

$8\frac{1}{9} + 1\frac{2}{9} = \underline{\qquad}$

$2\frac{3}{10} + 4\frac{2}{5} = \underline{\qquad}$

$3\frac{7}{12} + \frac{1}{4} = \underline{\qquad}$

$6\frac{1}{6} + 4\frac{2}{5} = \underline{\qquad}$

Let's Learn!

When you add mixed numbers, you might get an improper fraction in the sum. If this happens, you'll need to regroup! Try it with $1\frac{4}{5} + 3\frac{1}{2}$.

$1\frac{4}{5} + 3\frac{1}{2} = 4\frac{13}{10}$ Add the whole numbers, and then add the fractions using the LCD. The fraction in the sum, $\frac{13}{10}$, is improper.

$\frac{13}{10} = 1\frac{3}{10}$ Change the improper fraction into a mixed number.

$4 + 1\frac{3}{10} = 5\frac{3}{10}$ Then, add the whole numbers again to find the final answer.

Add. Write your answer as a mixed number in simplest form.

$4\frac{2}{3} + 2\frac{3}{4} = \underline{7\frac{5}{12}}$

$4\frac{8}{12} + 2\frac{9}{12} = 6\frac{17}{12} = 7\frac{5}{12}$

$7\frac{11}{12} + \frac{7}{12} = \underline{\hspace{2cm}}$

$3\frac{1}{2} + 1\frac{5}{8} = \underline{\hspace{2cm}}$

$5\frac{3}{4} + 3\frac{5}{6} = \underline{\hspace{2cm}}$

$4\frac{1}{3} + 4\frac{5}{7} = \underline{\hspace{2cm}}$

$8\frac{9}{10} + 3\frac{1}{4} = \underline{\hspace{2cm}}$

Add. Write your answer as a mixed number in simplest form.

$3\frac{1}{8} + 3\frac{1}{6} =$ _____

$7\frac{6}{7} + 4 =$ _____

$2\frac{1}{2} + 6\frac{5}{9} =$ _____

$5\frac{2}{3} + 8\frac{1}{4} =$ _____

$9\frac{4}{11} + \frac{4}{5} =$ _____

$4\frac{7}{10} + 3\frac{7}{10} =$ _____

$\frac{5}{8} + 11\frac{3}{4} =$ _____

$2\frac{3}{7} + 10\frac{2}{9} =$ _____

$7\frac{7}{10} + 9\frac{3}{8} =$ _____

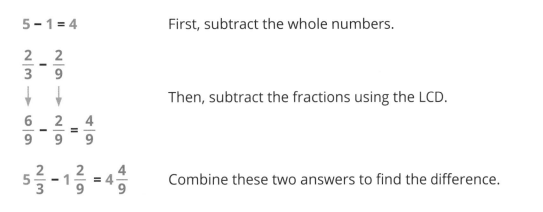

Let's Learn!

You can subtract mixed numbers by subtracting the whole numbers and then subtracting the fractions. Try it with $5\frac{2}{3} - 1\frac{2}{9}$.

$5 - 1 = 4$ First, subtract the whole numbers.

$\frac{2}{3} - \frac{2}{9}$

$\downarrow \quad \downarrow$ Then, subtract the fractions using the LCD.

$\frac{6}{9} - \frac{2}{9} = \frac{4}{9}$

$5\frac{2}{3} - 1\frac{2}{9} = 4\frac{4}{9}$ Combine these two answers to find the difference.

Subtract. Write your answer as a proper fraction or mixed number in simplest form.

$6\frac{4}{5} - 2\frac{1}{3} = \underline{4\frac{7}{15}}$

$6\frac{12}{15} - 2\frac{5}{15} = 4\frac{7}{15}$

$7\frac{9}{10} - 2\frac{3}{10} = \underline{\hspace{2cm}}$

$5\frac{5}{6} - 3\frac{1}{2} = \underline{\hspace{2cm}}$

$10\frac{7}{8} - 5\frac{1}{3} = \underline{\hspace{2cm}}$

$9\frac{3}{4} - 6\frac{2}{9} = \underline{\hspace{2cm}}$

$10\frac{11}{12} - \frac{5}{8} = \underline{\hspace{2cm}}$

Let's Learn!

To subtract mixed numbers, you might need to regroup. Try it with $5\frac{1}{2} - 3\frac{3}{4}$. First, use equivalent fractions to get the same denominator. Rewrite the problem as $5\frac{2}{4} - 3\frac{3}{4}$.

$5\frac{2}{4} - 3\frac{3}{4}$ You can't subtract $\frac{2}{4} - \frac{3}{4}$, so you need to regroup the $5\frac{2}{4}$.

$5\frac{2}{4} = 4\frac{4}{4} + \frac{2}{4} = 4\frac{6}{4}$ You can regroup one whole in $5\frac{2}{4}$ to get $4\frac{6}{4}$.

$4\frac{6}{4} - 3\frac{3}{4} = 1\frac{3}{4}$ Now you can subtract!

Subtract. Write your answer as a proper fraction or mixed number in simplest form.

$$4\frac{1}{4} - 1\frac{2}{3} = \underline{\ 2\frac{7}{12}\ }$$

$$4\frac{3}{12} - 1\frac{8}{12} = 3\frac{15}{12} - 1\frac{8}{12} = 2\frac{7}{12}$$

$$11\frac{1}{4} - \frac{3}{4} = \underline{\qquad}$$

$$7\frac{3}{8} - 1\frac{1}{2} = \underline{\qquad}$$

$$10 - 5\frac{4}{7} = \underline{\qquad}$$

$$8\frac{1}{6} - 2\frac{7}{12} = \underline{\qquad}$$

$$4\frac{1}{6} - 3\frac{5}{8} = \underline{\qquad}$$

Subtract. Write your answer as a proper fraction or mixed number in simplest form.

$11 \frac{1}{9} - 9 \frac{7}{9} = $ _____

$6 \frac{2}{5} - \frac{2}{3} = $ _____

$10 \frac{1}{4} - 5 \frac{5}{8} = $ _____

$8 \frac{5}{6} - 6 = $ _____

$9 \frac{3}{8} - 8 \frac{1}{12} = $ _____

$7 \frac{4}{7} - 3 \frac{1}{2} = $ _____

$15 \frac{3}{7} - 7 \frac{4}{5} = $ _____

$12 - 4 \frac{3}{4} = $ _____

$2 \frac{1}{5} - \frac{8}{11} = $ _____

Add or subtract. Write your answer as a proper fraction or mixed number in simplest form.

$4\frac{1}{5} + 3\frac{7}{10} =$ _____

$8\frac{1}{6} - 5\frac{5}{6} =$ _____

$2\frac{4}{7} + 6 =$ _____

$10\frac{1}{2} - \frac{3}{5} =$ _____

$11\frac{11}{12} - \frac{2}{3} =$ _____

$6\frac{4}{7} + 5\frac{1}{2} =$ _____

$12\frac{5}{6} - 9\frac{2}{3} =$ _____

$10 - 3\frac{7}{12} =$ _____

$8\frac{4}{5} + 7\frac{3}{4} =$ _____

$9\frac{1}{3} - 2\frac{2}{5} =$ _____

$5\frac{8}{9} + 9\frac{1}{6} =$ _____

Each number in the pyramid is the sum of the two numbers below it. Write the missing numbers as proper fractions or mixed numbers in simplest form.

Pyramid 1:
- Top: $9\frac{3}{10}$
- Middle: $5\frac{1}{2}$, $3\frac{4}{5}$
- Bottom: $3\frac{1}{5}$, $2\frac{3}{10}$, $1\frac{1}{2}$

Pyramid 2:
- Top: (blank)
- Middle: $5\frac{3}{8}$, $5\frac{3}{4}$
- Bottom: (blank), $2\frac{1}{4}$, (blank)

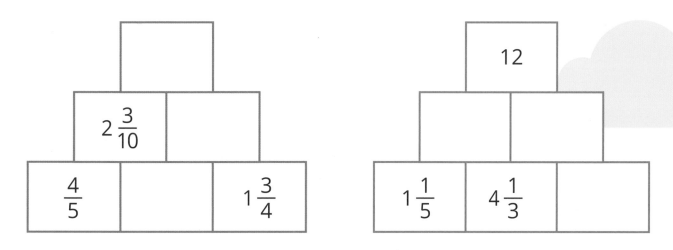

Pyramid 3:
- Top: (blank)
- Middle: $2\frac{3}{10}$, (blank)
- Bottom: $\frac{4}{5}$, (blank), $1\frac{3}{4}$

Pyramid 4:
- Top: 12
- Middle: (blank), (blank)
- Bottom: $1\frac{1}{5}$, $4\frac{1}{3}$, (blank)

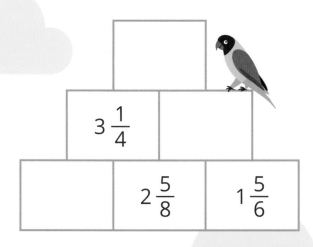

Pyramid 5:
- Top: (blank)
- Middle: $3\frac{1}{4}$, (blank)
- Bottom: (blank), $2\frac{5}{8}$, $1\frac{5}{6}$

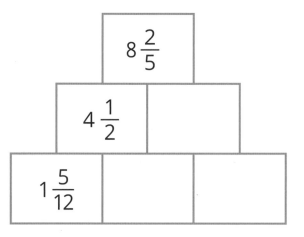

Pyramid 6:
- Top: $8\frac{2}{5}$
- Middle: $4\frac{1}{2}$, (blank)
- Bottom: $1\frac{5}{12}$, (blank), (blank)

Let's Learn!

To multiply a whole number by a fraction, multiply the whole number by the numerator. Keep the denominator the same! Try it with $4 \times \frac{2}{9}$.

$$4 \times \frac{2}{9} = \frac{4 \times 2}{9} = \frac{8}{9}$$

Multiply. Write your answer as a proper fraction or mixed number in simplest form.

$2 \times \frac{3}{8} =$ $\dfrac{6}{8} = \dfrac{3}{4}$

$3 \times \frac{1}{7} =$ _____

$8 \times \frac{1}{10} =$ _____

$\frac{1}{6} \times 3 =$ _____

$\frac{4}{5} \times 2 =$ _____

$2 \times \frac{5}{12} =$ _____

$9 \times \frac{3}{10} =$ _____

$\frac{3}{11} \times 8 =$ _____

$4 \times \frac{11}{12} =$ _____

$6 \times \frac{7}{8} =$ _____

Multiply. Write your answer as a proper fraction or mixed number in simplest form.

$7 \times \dfrac{1}{2} =$ _____

$8 \times \dfrac{1}{6} =$ _____

$9 \times \dfrac{3}{8} =$ _____

$\dfrac{11}{12} \times 5 =$ _____

$\dfrac{2}{3} \times 6 =$ _____

$\dfrac{3}{4} \times 2 =$ _____

$4 \times \dfrac{7}{12} =$ _____

$3 \times \dfrac{5}{6} =$ _____

$\dfrac{3}{10} \times 6 =$ _____

$\dfrac{4}{5} \times 10 =$ _____

$7 \times \dfrac{5}{9} =$ _____

$8 \times \dfrac{10}{11} =$ _____

$\dfrac{5}{6} \times 12 =$ _____

$14 \times \dfrac{6}{7} =$ _____

Let's Learn!

To multiply two fractions, multiply the numerators and multiply the denominators. Try it with $\frac{2}{7} \times \frac{1}{3}$.

$$\frac{2}{7} \times \frac{1}{3} = \frac{2 \times 1}{7 \times 3} = \frac{2}{21}$$

Multiply. Write your answer in simplest form.

$\frac{1}{6} \times \frac{2}{3} = \frac{2}{18} = \frac{1}{9}$

$\frac{5}{9} \times \frac{1}{3} =$ _____

$\frac{6}{7} \times \frac{1}{2} =$ _____

$\frac{3}{5} \times \frac{1}{2} =$ _____

$\frac{2}{5} \times \frac{7}{9} =$ _____

$\frac{2}{3} \times \frac{3}{8} =$ _____

$\frac{1}{4} \times \frac{5}{6} =$ _____

$\frac{1}{12} \times \frac{3}{4} =$ _____

$\frac{9}{10} \times \frac{2}{10} =$ _____

$\frac{9}{10} \times \frac{9}{10} =$ _____

IXL.com skill ID 8KV

DIG DEEPER! Look at the bottom two problems on the page. Which one is equal to $\left(\frac{9}{10}\right)^2$?

Multiplying fractions

Multiply. Write your answer in simplest form. Then circle all of the answers that are greater than $\frac{1}{2}$.

$\frac{3}{8} \times \frac{1}{2} =$ _____

$\frac{5}{7} \times \frac{1}{3} =$ _____

$\frac{3}{10} \times \frac{2}{3} =$ _____

$\frac{1}{4} \times \frac{1}{5} =$ _____

$\frac{1}{2} \times \frac{5}{12} =$ _____

$\frac{4}{5} \times \frac{2}{3} =$ _____

$\frac{3}{4} \times \frac{3}{4} =$ _____

$\frac{7}{9} \times \frac{1}{2} =$ _____

$\frac{5}{8} \times \frac{1}{4} =$ _____

$\frac{5}{9} \times \frac{3}{5} =$ _____

$\frac{7}{8} \times \frac{4}{5} =$ _____

$\frac{5}{11} \times \frac{11}{12} =$ _____

IXL.com
skill ID
S6G

Let's Learn!

If you have a **fraction of a number**, you can multiply to find that amount.

$$\frac{2}{7} \text{ of } 3 = \frac{2}{7} \times 3 = \frac{6}{7}$$

Multiply. Write your answer as a proper fraction or mixed number in simplest form.

$\frac{1}{8}$ of 6 = _____

$\frac{2}{3}$ of 4 = _____

$\frac{4}{9}$ of 3 = _____

$\frac{3}{4}$ of 8 = _____

Keep going! Multiply. Write your answer as a proper fraction or mixed number in simplest form.

$\frac{1}{2}$ of $\frac{1}{5}$ = _____

$\frac{5}{6}$ of $\frac{1}{8}$ = _____

$\frac{2}{3}$ of $\frac{3}{7}$ = _____

$\frac{5}{12}$ of $\frac{3}{5}$ = _____

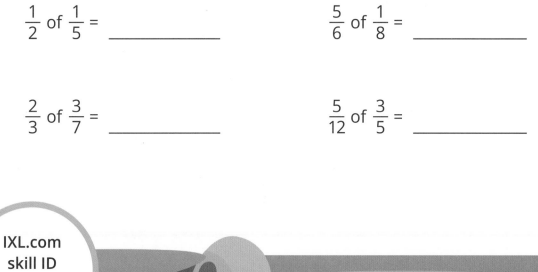

IXL.com
skill ID
AHX

Answer each question. Write your answer as a proper fraction or mixed number in simplest form.

Anna is making signs for a yard sale in her neighborhood. She needs to make 10 signs. So far, she has completed $\frac{2}{5}$ of the signs. How many signs has she made so far?

_____

At Pine Time Summer Camp, 12 campers sign up to go swimming. Of the 12 campers, $\frac{2}{3}$ of them are advanced swimmers. How many of these campers are advanced swimmers?

_____

Jackson and his teammates are doing exercises at the end of soccer practice. They have $\frac{1}{2}$ of an hour to do leg lunges and sprints. If they do leg lunges for $\frac{1}{2}$ of the time, how long is that?

_____

Last Saturday, $\frac{3}{4}$ of the animals at Anderson's Animal Clinic were dogs. Of these dogs, $\frac{1}{6}$ were small dogs. What fraction of the animals at the clinic were small dogs?

_____

Let's Learn!

To multiply a mixed number by a fraction, rewrite the mixed number as an improper fraction. Then multiply across. Try it with $2\frac{1}{3} \times \frac{2}{5}$. Start by writing $2\frac{1}{3}$ as an improper fraction.

$$2\frac{1}{3} = \frac{7}{3} \longrightarrow \frac{7}{3} \times \frac{2}{5} = \frac{14}{15}$$

Multiply. Write your answer as a proper fraction or mixed number in simplest form.

$1\frac{1}{4} \times \frac{5}{6} = \underline{\ 1\frac{1}{24}\ }$

$\frac{5}{4} \times \frac{5}{6} = \frac{25}{24} = 1\frac{1}{24}$

$\frac{1}{5} \times 1\frac{1}{6} = \underline{\hspace{2cm}}$

$4\frac{1}{2} \times \frac{3}{8} = \underline{\hspace{2cm}}$

$3\frac{2}{3} \times \frac{3}{4} = \underline{\hspace{2cm}}$

$3\frac{3}{4} \times \frac{3}{5} = \underline{\hspace{2cm}}$

$\frac{5}{9} \times 2\frac{4}{5} = \underline{\hspace{2cm}}$

$\frac{2}{3} \times 6\frac{1}{3} = \underline{\hspace{2cm}}$

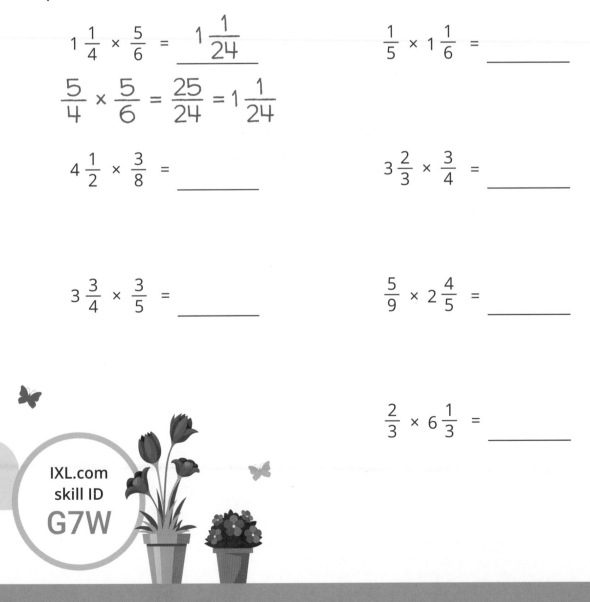

IXL.com
skill ID
G7W

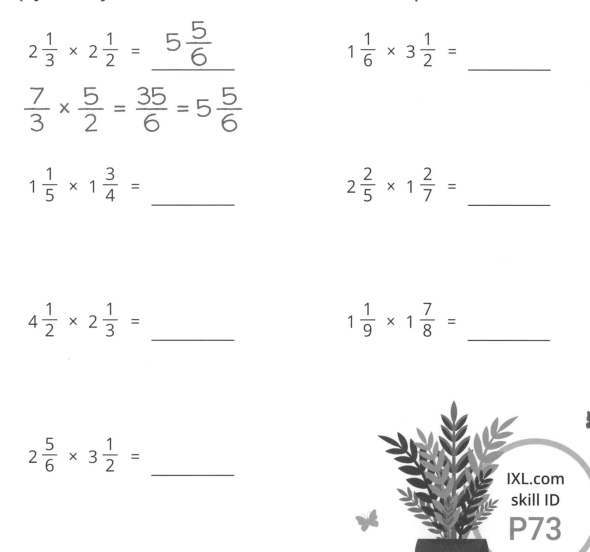

Let's Learn!

To multiply two mixed numbers, rewrite both mixed numbers as improper fractions. Then multiply across and write your answer as a mixed number. Try it with $1\frac{1}{2} \times 1\frac{1}{4}$.

$$1\frac{1}{2} \times 1\frac{1}{4} = \frac{3}{2} \times \frac{5}{4} = \frac{15}{8} \longrightarrow \frac{15}{8} = 1\frac{7}{8}$$

Multiply. Write your answer as a mixed number in simplest form.

$2\frac{1}{3} \times 2\frac{1}{2} = \underline{\quad 5\frac{5}{6} \quad}$

$\frac{7}{3} \times \frac{5}{2} = \frac{35}{6} = 5\frac{5}{6}$

$1\frac{1}{6} \times 3\frac{1}{2} = \underline{\qquad}$

$1\frac{1}{5} \times 1\frac{3}{4} = \underline{\qquad}$

$2\frac{2}{5} \times 1\frac{2}{7} = \underline{\qquad}$

$4\frac{1}{2} \times 2\frac{1}{3} = \underline{\qquad}$

$1\frac{1}{9} \times 1\frac{7}{8} = \underline{\qquad}$

$2\frac{5}{6} \times 3\frac{1}{2} = \underline{\qquad}$

IXL.com
skill ID
P73

Time to review! Multiply. Write your answer as a proper fraction or mixed number in simplest form.

$4 \times \dfrac{3}{5} =$ _____

$\dfrac{1}{2} \times \dfrac{1}{3} =$ _____

$\dfrac{7}{8} \times \dfrac{1}{4} =$ _____

$\dfrac{5}{9} \times 5 =$ _____

$2\dfrac{1}{2} \times 3 =$ _____

$2\dfrac{1}{9} \times \dfrac{1}{4} =$ _____

$\dfrac{3}{5} \times 1\dfrac{2}{3} =$ _____

$\dfrac{9}{10} \times 2\dfrac{1}{4} =$ _____

$3\dfrac{1}{5} \times 4 =$ _____

$4\dfrac{1}{2} \times 1\dfrac{3}{10} =$ _____

$1\dfrac{2}{7} \times 4\dfrac{1}{5} =$ _____

IXL.com
skill ID
6Q4

Find the path from start to finish! Step only on spaces that have products between 1 and 2. No diagonal moves are allowed.

START

$\frac{1}{4} \times 5$	$3\frac{1}{2} \times \frac{1}{3}$	$4 \times \frac{2}{5}$	$2\frac{1}{3} \times \frac{7}{8}$
$3\frac{1}{2} \times \frac{5}{6}$	$\frac{1}{2} \times \frac{1}{5}$	$1\frac{1}{8} \times 1\frac{1}{2}$	$2 \times \frac{1}{3}$
$5 \times \frac{3}{5}$	$\frac{7}{10} \times \frac{1}{4}$	$2\frac{1}{10} \times \frac{5}{7}$	$3\frac{3}{4} \times \frac{1}{8}$
$\frac{1}{2} \times \frac{6}{7}$	$1 \times 1\frac{1}{12}$	$\frac{3}{8} \times 3$	$4 \times \frac{5}{8}$
$1\frac{1}{2} \times 1\frac{2}{3}$	$4\frac{1}{5} \times \frac{2}{7}$	$\frac{7}{10} \times 5$	$\frac{7}{8} \times \frac{3}{4}$
$4\frac{1}{8} \times \frac{7}{10}$	$3 \times \frac{5}{12}$	$1\frac{1}{10} \times \frac{11}{12}$	$2\frac{1}{2} \times \frac{3}{5}$

FINISH

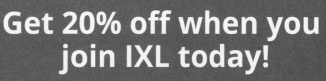

Answer each question. Write your answer as a proper fraction or mixed number in simplest form.

Adrian is making a blue cheese dip for a party snack. Here is the recipe he will use:

Recipe: Blue Cheese Dip
Ingredients

1 2/3 cups mayonnaise   3 teaspoons dried parsley

1/2 cup blue cheese   1/8 teaspoon garlic salt

1 1/4 cups chopped green onions   Optional:

1 3/4 cups sour cream   1 1/2 cups chopped fresh dill

Adrian decides to double the amount of garlic salt. How much garlic salt does he use?

_____

He also doubles the amount of green onions. How many cups does he use?

_____

Adrian measures out $\frac{1}{3}$ of the dried parsley. How much does he measure?

_____

IXL.com
skill ID
QHN

Adrian wants to add some chopped fresh dill. He decides to add $\frac{1}{2}$ of the recommended amount. How much dill does he add?

_____

Answer each question. Write your answer as a proper fraction or mixed number in simplest form.

On Wednesday, Mark ran $3\frac{3}{5}$ miles at cross country practice. At Thursday's practice, he ran $2\frac{1}{2}$ times as far as he did on Wednesday. How many miles did he run on Thursday?

_____

Justin bought 4 packages of cheese at Carly's Cheese Shop. Each package of cheese weighed $1\frac{1}{4}$ pounds. How many pounds of cheese did he buy?

_____

Gavin has $3\frac{1}{2}$ cups of vegetable oil in his cupboard. He needs $\frac{1}{2}$ of the oil for a salad dressing. How many cups of oil does he need for the salad dressing?

_____

Mackenzie's apartment is $5\frac{1}{2}$ blocks from her work. If she walks to work and then back home, how many blocks has she walked?

_____

IXL.com
skill ID
5W6

Exploration Zone

MULTIPLICATION AS SCALING

When you multiply, the answer is often bigger than the number you started with. But not always! Try it yourself. Solve the problems below. Then determine if the product is greater than, less than, or equal to 4.

$4 \times \dfrac{1}{9} =$ ___$\dfrac{4}{9}$___　　The product is ___LESS THAN___ 4.

$4 \times 1\dfrac{1}{3} =$ _____　　The product is _____ 4.

$4 \times 1 =$ _____　　The product is _____ 4.

Look at the second factor in each of the problems above. Is that factor greater than 1, less than 1, or equal to 1? Can you come up with a rule to predict the size of each product?

IXL.com
skill ID
Q7M

TRY IT YOURSELF!

Without doing the math, compare each pair using > or <.

$10 \times 2\dfrac{4}{5}$ (>) 10 　　　　 $\dfrac{5}{6} \times \dfrac{1}{10}$ ◯ $\dfrac{5}{6}$

$9 \times \dfrac{2}{3}$ ◯ 9 　　　　 $\dfrac{3}{5} \times 2\dfrac{1}{9}$ ◯ $\dfrac{3}{5}$

You can divide a whole number by a fraction using a model. Try it with $2 \div \frac{1}{5}$.

Start by breaking 2 wholes into $\frac{1}{5}$ pieces.

Count the number of $\frac{1}{5}$ pieces. There are 10 pieces, so $2 \div \frac{1}{5} = 10$.

Divide. Use the models to help.

$3 \div \frac{1}{3} = \underline{\ 9\ }$

$4 \div \frac{1}{2} = \underline{\hspace{2em}}$

$2 \div \frac{1}{4} = \underline{\hspace{2em}}$

$3 \div \frac{1}{6} = \underline{\hspace{2em}}$

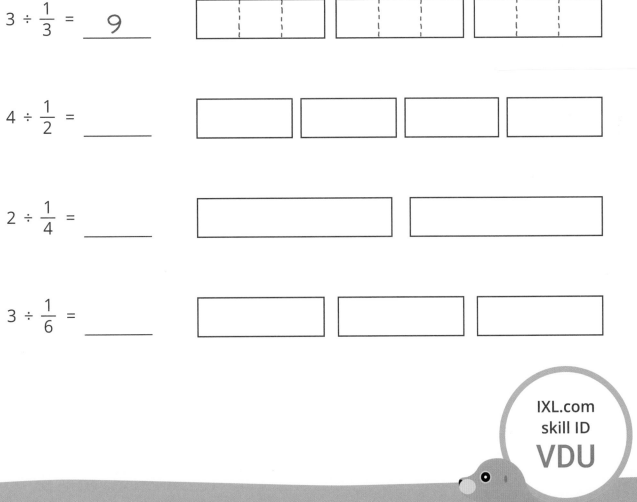

Let's Learn!

You can divide a fraction by a whole number, too. Try it with $\frac{1}{4} \div 3$.

Start with a model of $\frac{1}{4}$. Divide the $\frac{1}{4}$ piece into 3 pieces. What fraction of the whole is each new piece?

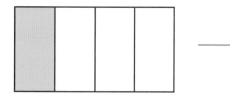 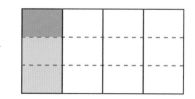

Each new piece is $\frac{1}{12}$ of the whole. So, $\frac{1}{4} \div 3 = \frac{1}{12}$.

Divide. Use the models to help.

$\frac{1}{5} \div 2 = \underline{\frac{1}{10}}$

$\frac{1}{3} \div 4 = \underline{\hspace{2cm}}$

$\frac{1}{6} \div 3 = \underline{\hspace{2cm}}$

$\frac{1}{4} \div 2 = \underline{\hspace{2cm}}$

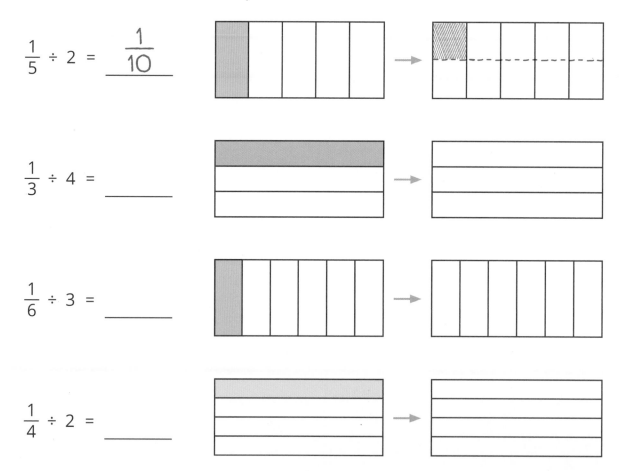

Divide. Draw models to help.

$4 \div \dfrac{1}{5} =$ _20_

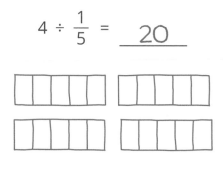

$\dfrac{1}{4} \div 5 =$ _$\dfrac{1}{20}$_

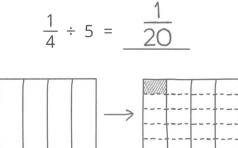

$2 \div \dfrac{1}{6} =$ _____

$\dfrac{1}{2} \div 6 =$ _____

$3 \div \dfrac{1}{5} =$ _____

$\dfrac{1}{3} \div 5 =$ _____

$5 \div \dfrac{1}{2} =$ _____

$\dfrac{1}{5} \div 2 =$ _____

IXL.com
skill ID
A7W

Answer each question. Draw models to help.

Erica made a block of scented soap. The block weighs $\frac{1}{2}$ of a pound. If she cuts the soap into 2 equal bars, how much will each bar weigh?

_____

Bailey bought 2 bags of pita chips. If she eats $\frac{1}{7}$ of a bag each day, how long will the chips last?

_____

Mr. Murray bought $\frac{1}{4}$ of a pound of turkey at the deli. He wants to use the turkey to make 3 sandwiches. If he splits the turkey equally, how much turkey will be on each sandwich?

_____

Zander wants to make a few bandanas for his puppy. He has 3 yards of paw-print fabric. Each bandana uses $\frac{1}{2}$ of a yard of fabric. How many bandanas can he make?

_____

IXL.com
skill ID
G2N

For more practice, visit IXL.com or the IXL mobile app and enter this code in the search bar.

Let's Learn!

To divide fractions without models, you can use a **reciprocal**. You can find the reciprocal of a fraction by switching the numerator and the denominator. For example, the reciprocal of $\frac{3}{4}$ is $\frac{4}{3}$.

$$\frac{3}{4} \rightarrow \frac{4}{3}$$

You can also find the reciprocal of a whole number. To start, write the whole number as a fraction by placing it over 1. Then switch the numerator and denominator. So, the reciprocal of 5 is $\frac{1}{5}$.

$$5 = \frac{5}{1} \rightarrow \frac{1}{5}$$

Find the reciprocal.

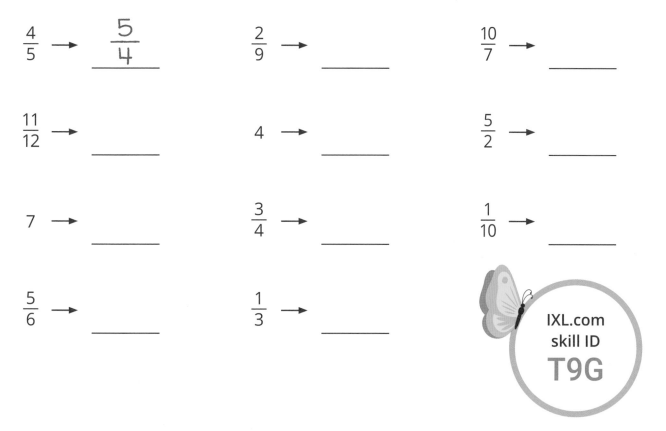

$\frac{4}{5} \rightarrow \frac{5}{4}$

$\frac{2}{9} \rightarrow$ _____

$\frac{10}{7} \rightarrow$ _____

$\frac{11}{12} \rightarrow$ _____

$4 \rightarrow$ _____

$\frac{5}{2} \rightarrow$ _____

$7 \rightarrow$ _____

$\frac{3}{4} \rightarrow$ _____

$\frac{1}{10} \rightarrow$ _____

$\frac{5}{6} \rightarrow$ _____

$\frac{1}{3} \rightarrow$ _____

IXL.com
skill ID
T9G

Let's Learn!

Dividing by a fraction is the same as multiplying by its reciprocal!
Try it with $\frac{2}{5} \div \frac{1}{2}$. Rewrite the division problem using multiplication.
Write the fraction $\frac{1}{2}$ as its reciprocal, $\frac{2}{1}$. Then multiply across.

$$\frac{2}{5} \div \frac{1}{2} \longrightarrow \frac{2}{5} \times \frac{2}{1} = \frac{4}{5}$$

When you divide by a whole number, that is also the same as multiplying by
its reciprocal. Try it with $\frac{3}{4} \div 5$. Remember that the reciprocal of 5 is $\frac{1}{5}$.

$$\frac{3}{4} \div 5 \longrightarrow \frac{3}{4} \times \frac{1}{5} = \frac{3}{20}$$

Divide. Write your answer as a proper fraction or mixed number in simplest form.

$\frac{3}{4} \div \frac{2}{3} = \dfrac{\frac{3}{4} \times \frac{3}{2} = \frac{9}{8} = 1\frac{1}{8}}{}$ $\frac{2}{5} \div \frac{1}{6} = \underline{\hspace{4cm}}$

$\frac{6}{7} \div 3 = \underline{\hspace{4cm}}$ $\frac{1}{4} \div \frac{8}{9} = \underline{\hspace{4cm}}$

$\frac{5}{8} \div \frac{1}{2} = \underline{\hspace{4cm}}$ $2 \div \frac{1}{3} = \underline{\hspace{4cm}}$

$\frac{9}{10} \div \frac{4}{5} = \underline{\hspace{4cm}}$ $\frac{11}{12} \div 4 = \underline{\hspace{4cm}}$

Divide. Write your answer as a proper fraction or mixed number in simplest form.

$\dfrac{2}{9} \div \dfrac{1}{3} =$ _____

$\dfrac{1}{2} \div \dfrac{5}{7} =$ _____

$4 \div \dfrac{3}{4} =$ _____

$\dfrac{5}{6} \div \dfrac{1}{4} =$ _____

$\dfrac{3}{7} \div \dfrac{1}{5} =$ _____

$\dfrac{8}{9} \div 5 =$ _____

$8 \div \dfrac{2}{3} =$ _____

$\dfrac{3}{10} \div \dfrac{1}{4} =$ _____

$\dfrac{3}{5} \div \dfrac{2}{7} =$ _____

$\dfrac{4}{9} \div \dfrac{2}{5} =$ _____

CHECK IT OUT! | Go back to pages 135 and 136. Try solving the problems using a reciprocal. The answers should be the same!

IXL.com
skill ID
GL6

Let's Learn!

When you divide two whole numbers, you can show your answer as a fraction! For example, you can show $8 \div 24$ as $\frac{8}{24}$. Then simplify from there!

$$8 \div 24 = \frac{8}{24} = \frac{1}{3}$$

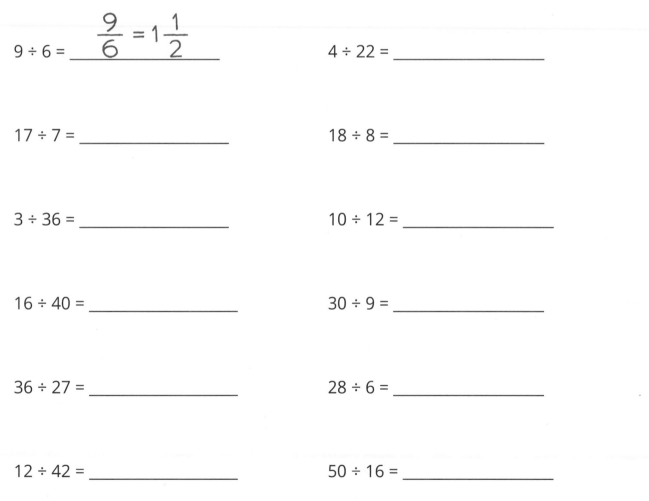

Divide. Write your answer as a proper fraction or mixed number in simplest form.

$9 \div 6 = \dfrac{9}{6} = 1\dfrac{1}{2}$

$4 \div 22 = $ _____

$17 \div 7 = $ _____

$18 \div 8 = $ _____

$3 \div 36 = $ _____

$10 \div 12 = $ _____

$16 \div 40 = $ _____

$30 \div 9 = $ _____

$36 \div 27 = $ _____

$28 \div 6 = $ _____

$12 \div 42 = $ _____

$50 \div 16 = $ _____

Answer each question. Write your answer as a proper fraction or mixed number in simplest form.

Kelly split 2 pounds of flour equally between 6 different muffin recipes. How many pounds of flour did she use for each recipe?

_____

The candy maker at The Fudge Nudge made 10 pounds of chocolate fudge. If he cuts the fudge into 40 equal-sized samples, how much will each sample weigh?

_____

Elijah volunteered at the Harrodsburg Animal Shelter on Saturday. He used a 12-pound bag of dog food to feed 20 large dogs. If each dog was fed the same amount, how many pounds of food did each dog receive?

_____

Last week, Jessie taught 10 cycling classes at Spin City. She taught for 15 hours in all. If each cycling class was the same length, how long was each class?

_____

In a 6-pack of Purr-fect Portions, there are 33 ounces of cat food. If each can of food holds the same amount, how many ounces are in each can?

_____

IXL.com
skill ID
CTD

Let's Learn!

A **sequence** is a list of numbers that follows a pattern or rule. The numbers in a sequence are the **terms**. Look at the example below.

$$0, \ 4, \ 8, \ 12, \ 16$$

+ 4   + 4   + 4   + 4

To get from one term to the next, you add 4. So, the rule for this sequence is to add 4!

Use the rule to fill in the missing terms.

Rule: subtract 12	87	75			

Rule: add 9	10	19			

Rule: multiply by 2	3	6			

Rule: subtract 75	500			275	

Rule: multiply by 3	1		9		

IXL.com
skill ID
RPP

Use the rule to fill in the missing terms.

Rule: multiply by 2, then add 1	3	7			

Rule: add 3, then multiply by 2	17	40			

Rule: add 1, then multiply by 2	100	202			

Rule: subtract 50, then multiply by 2	120	140			

Rule: multiply by 3, then subtract 5	3	4		16	

Rule: add 8, then multiply by 3	10		186		1,770

Rule: multiply by 2, then add 10	5			110	

CHALLENGE ZONE

Use the rule to fill in the missing terms. Write all fraction sequences with proper fractions and mixed numbers in simplest form.

Rule: add 0.8	1.1	1.9	2.7	3.5	4.3

Rule: subtract 2.5	20.3	17.8			10.3

Rule: add $\frac{1}{2}$	$\frac{1}{5}$	$\frac{7}{10}$		$1\frac{7}{10}$	

Rule: subtract $\frac{1}{6}$	$\frac{11}{12}$		$\frac{7}{12}$		

Rule: multiply by 0.5	100.8	50.4			

Rule: multiply by $1\frac{1}{2}$	$1\frac{1}{3}$		3		

Rule: add $1\frac{3}{4}$	$\frac{1}{6}$			$5\frac{5}{12}$	

Find the rule. Then use the rule to fill in the missing terms.

Rule: ADD 15	35	50	65	80	95

Rule:	83	72	61		

Rule:	1	4	16		

Rule:	7	14	28		

Rule:	150	137	124		

Rule:	3	15	75		

Rule:	111	222	333		

IXL.com
skill ID
GM2

Exploration Zone

TRIANGULAR NUMBERS

Some sequences follow special patterns! One example is the sequence of **triangular numbers.** You can make this sequence by drawing triangles made up of dots. Start with one dot, and then add a new row of dots below as you go.

Try drawing the next triangular number below!

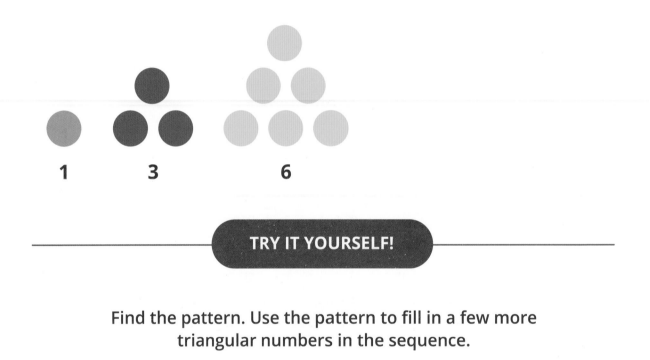

TRY IT YOURSELF!

Find the pattern. Use the pattern to fill in a few more triangular numbers in the sequence.

1, 3, 6, 10, 15, 21,_____, _____, _____

+2   +3

SQUARE NUMBERS

Square numbers make up another special sequence. To make this sequence, start with one square. Then add another row and another column of squares for every step!

Can you draw the next square number?

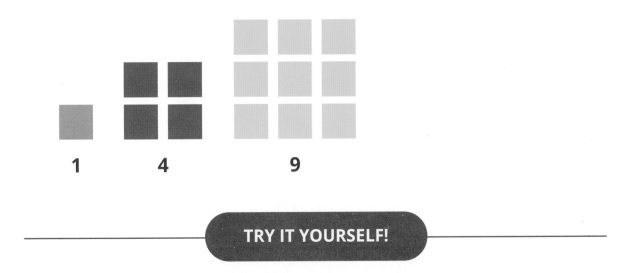

1   4   9

TRY IT YOURSELF!

Find the pattern. Use the pattern to fill in a few more square numbers in the sequence.

1, 4, 9, 16, 25, 36, _____, _____, _____, _____

+3   +5

The **coordinate plane** is the grid formed by the intersection of horizontal and vertical number lines.

The **x-axis** is the horizontal number line. The **y-axis** is the vertical number line. The two axes meet at zero, or **the origin**.

An **ordered pair (x, y)** tells the location of a point on the coordinate plane.

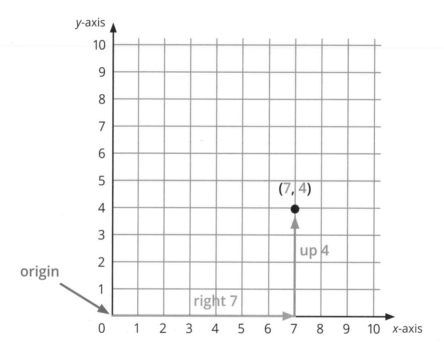

The first number in the ordered pair is called the **x-coordinate**. The second number is called the **y-coordinate**.

In the ordered pair (7, 4), the x-coordinate is 7 and the y-coordinate is 4. From the origin, the point is 7 units to the right and 4 units up.

Write the ordered pair for each point.

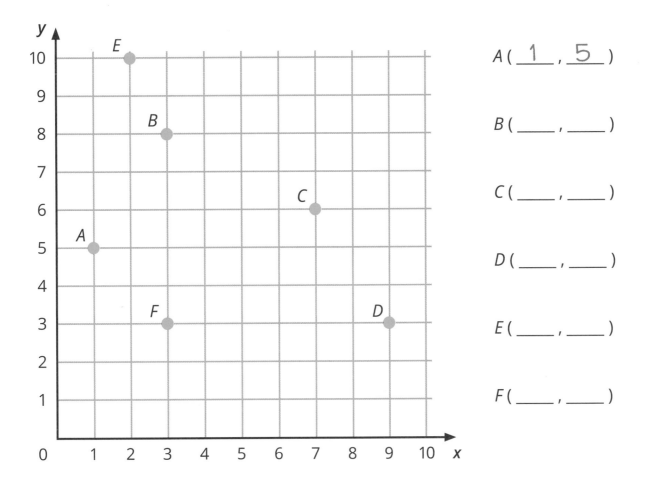

A (__1__ , __5__)

B (____ , ____)

C (____ , ____)

D (____ , ____)

E (____ , ____)

F (____ , ____)

IXL.com
skill ID
NTR

When you draw a point on a coordinate plane, you are *plotting* the point! Plot and label the points.

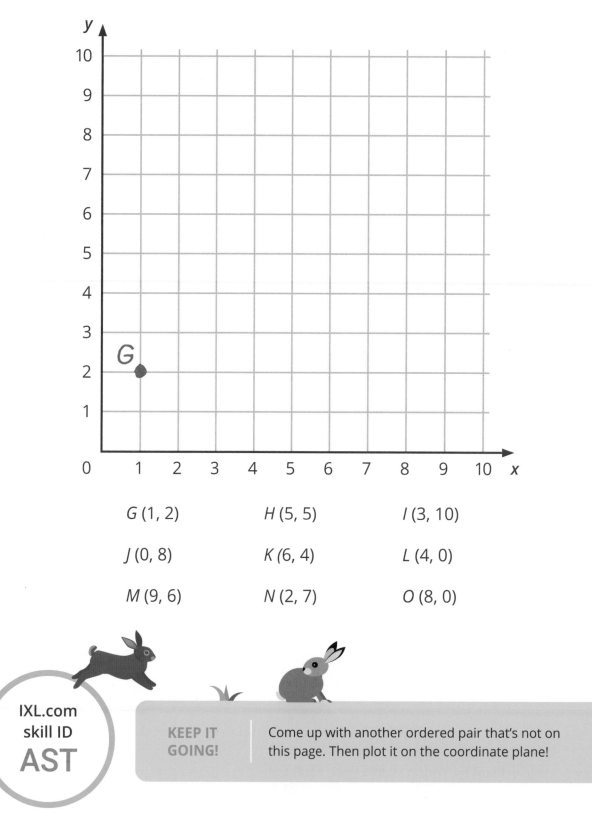

G (1, 2)   H (5, 5)   I (3, 10)

J (0, 8)   K (6, 4)   L (4, 0)

M (9, 6)   N (2, 7)   O (8, 0)

IXL.com
skill ID
AST

KEEP IT GOING! Come up with another ordered pair that's not on this page. Then plot it on the coordinate plane!

You can move a point up, down, right, or left on a graph. This movement is called a *translation*. Try it yourself! Move each point. Then write the new ordered pair.

Move point *P* down 5 units.

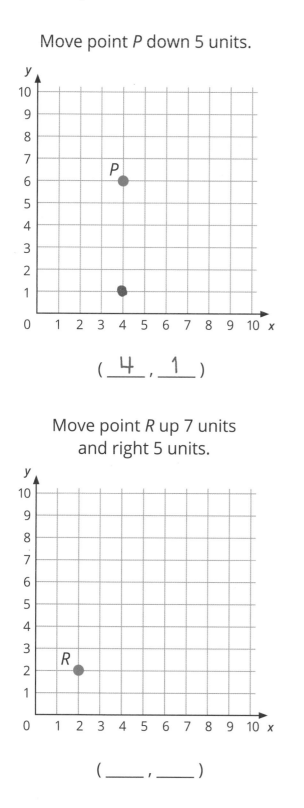

(__4__ , __1__)

Move point *W* right 2 units.

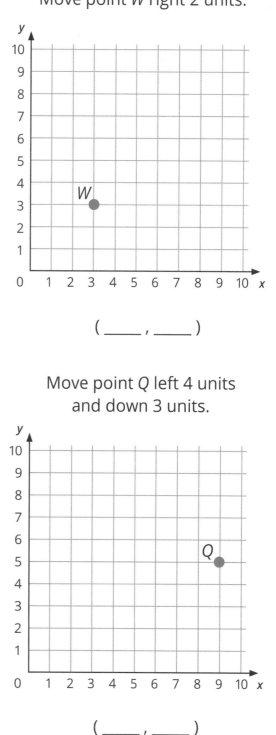

(_____ , _____)

Move point *R* up 7 units and right 5 units.

(_____ , _____)

Move point *Q* left 4 units and down 3 units.

(_____ , _____)

If two points are on the same line, you can find the distance between the points. Just count the number of units between them! Try it yourself. Find the distance between the points.

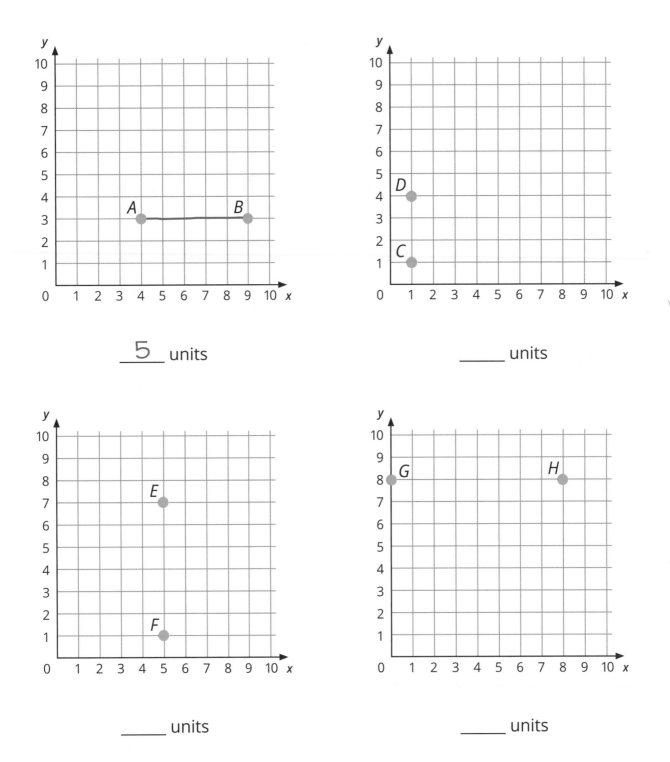

_____5_____ units

_____ units

_____ units

_____ units

The coordinate plane below shows a map. Use the map to answer the questions.

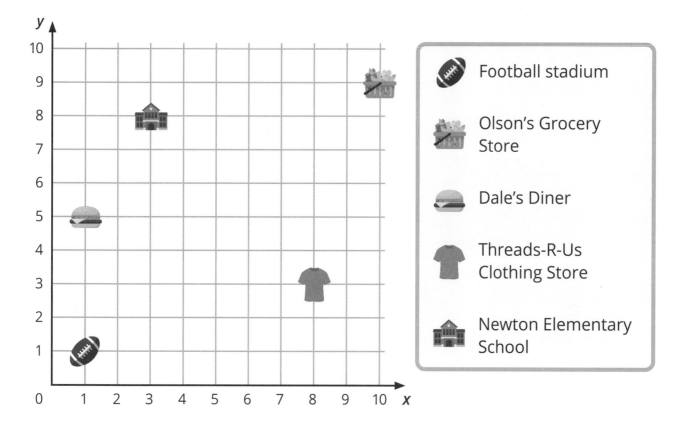

What is the location of Olson's Grocery Store? Write the ordered pair.

_____

What is located at (8, 3)?

_____

What is the distance, in units, between the foodball stadium and Dale's Diner?

_____

If you go left 1 and up 3 from Threads-R-Us clothing store, you will find the city library. Plot and label this point on the coordinate plane.

IXL.com
skill ID
ZBD

Look at the map of Big Top Amusement Park. Use the map to answer the questions.

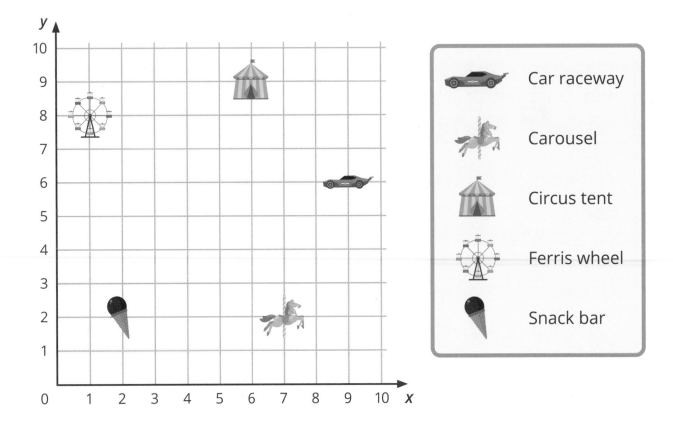

What is the location of the car raceway? Write the ordered pair.

_____

What is the distance, in units, between the carousel and the snack bar?

_____

If you go down 2 from the circus tent, you will find the information booth. What is the location of the information booth? Write the ordered pair.

_____

The bumper-boat ride is located at (4, 5). Plot and label this point on the coordinate plane.

In the tables below, each row shows an ordered pair. The first column has the *x*-coordinate, and the second column has the *y*-coordinate. Plot the points from each table on the coordinate plane. The first point has been done for you.

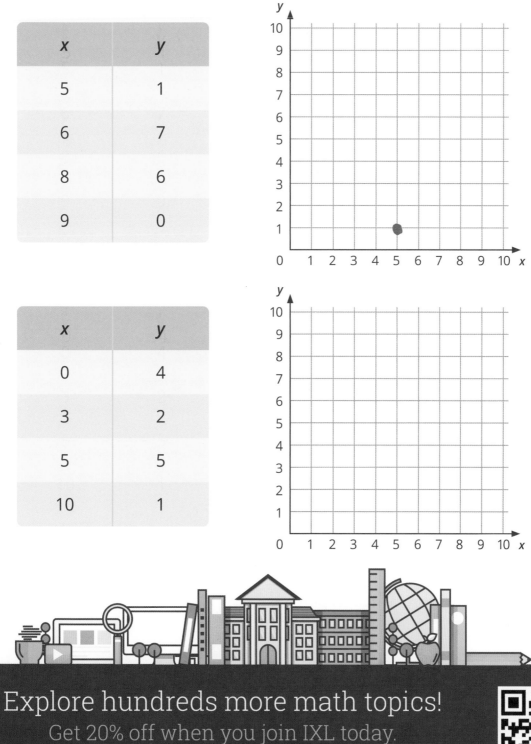

x	y
5	1
6	7
8	6
9	0

x	y
0	4
3	2
5	5
10	1

A **line graph** connects points to show change over time. Answer each question using the line graph.

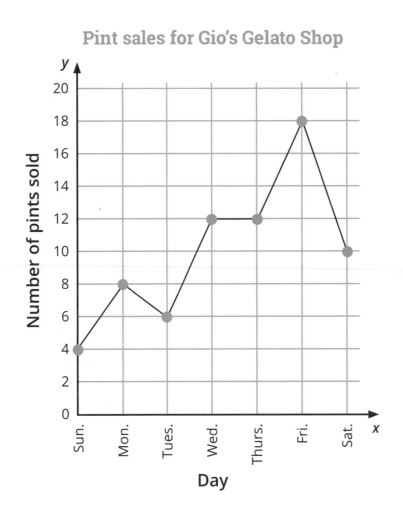

Pint sales for Gio's Gelato Shop

Last week, Gio tracked the number of pints that his shop sold each day. How many pints did his shop sell on Tuesday?   _____

On which day did his shop sell exactly 10 pints of gelato?   _____

On which day did his shop sell the most pints of gelato?   _____

On which day did his shop sell the fewest pints of gelato?   _____

Answer each question using the line graph.

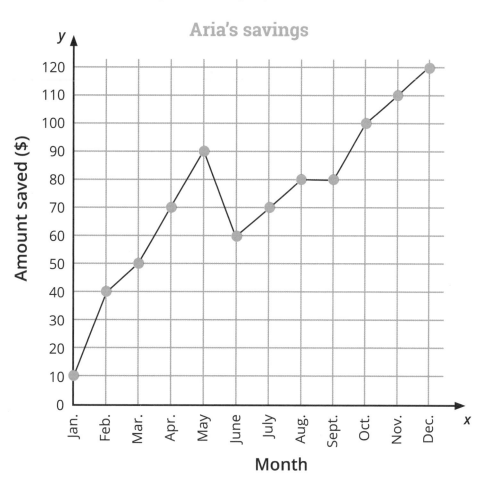

Aria recorded the amount of money in her bank account at the beginning of each month. How much money was in her bank account at the beginning of April?

_____

During which month did she take money out of her bank account?

_____

During which month did her bank account stay at the same amount?

_____

Aria took $20 out of her bank account during the month of December. How much money was left in her account?

_____

Circle the best estimate for the measurement of each object.

Length of a toothbrush

(5 inches)   5 feet

Length of a couch

7 inches   7 feet

Weight of an adult dog

25 ounces   25 pounds

Width of a kitchen table

40 inches   40 yards

Height of a house

30 feet   30 miles

Capacity of a water bottle

20 fluid ounces   20 quarts

Circle the object that best matches the measurement.

6 inches

Length of a desk

(Length of a pen)

1 pound

Weight of a squirrel

Weight of a tiger

2 tons

Weight of a car

Weight of a bicycle

6 feet

Height of a Ferris wheel

Height of a person

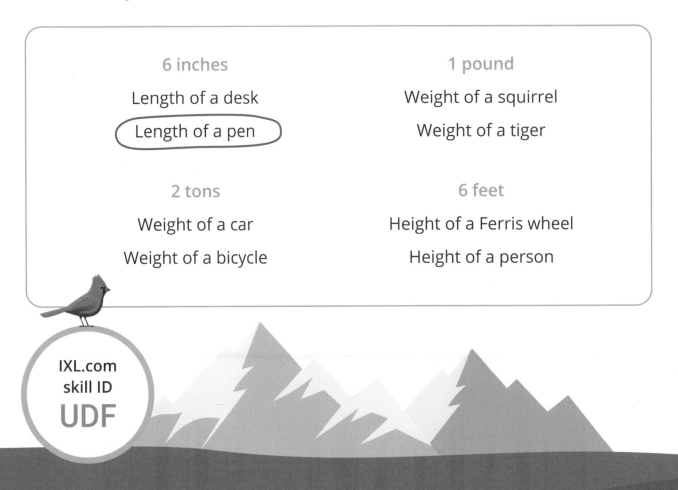

IXL.com
skill ID

UDF

Let's Learn!

You can measure the length of an object using **customary units of length**. This table shows some of these units and the relationships between them.

Customary units of length
1 foot (ft.) = 12 inches (in.)
1 yard (yd.) = 3 ft.
1 mile (mi.) = 1,760 yd.

To convert between units, you can multiply or divide! For example, try converting 9 feet to inches or yards.

9 feet × 12 inches per foot = 108 inches

9 feet ÷ 3 feet per yard = 3 yards

So, 9 feet is the same as 108 inches or 3 yards.

Convert each measurement.

5 yd. = _____15_____ ft.

$5 \times 3 = 15$

36 in. = _____ ft.

24 ft. = _____ yd.

2 mi. = _____ yd.

$\frac{1}{2}$ ft. = _____ in.

$2 \frac{1}{3}$ yd. = _____ ft.

IXL.com
skill ID
7E8

Let's Learn!

Sometimes when you divide to convert measurements, you get a remainder. You can use the remainder to write the answer. Try converting 17 inches to feet.

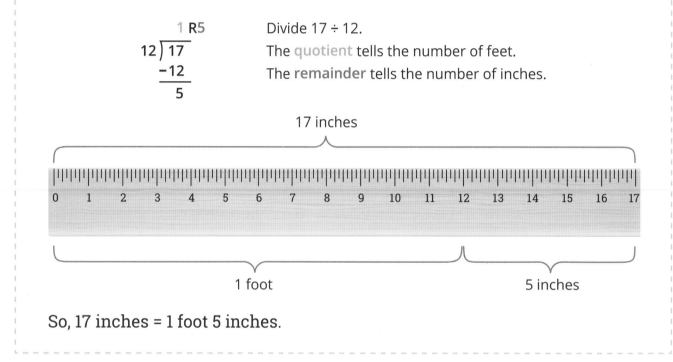

$$\begin{array}{r} 1 \text{ R5} \\ 12\overline{)17} \\ -12 \\ \hline 5 \end{array}$$

Divide 17 ÷ 12.

The quotient tells the number of feet.

The remainder tells the number of inches.

17 inches

1 foot   5 inches

So, 17 inches = 1 foot 5 inches.

Convert each measurement.

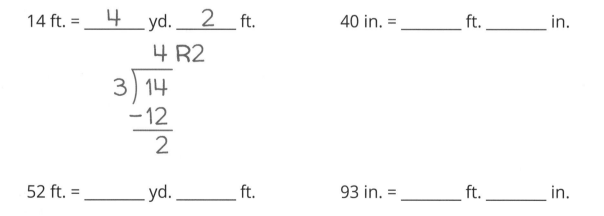

14 ft. = ___4___ yd. ___2___ ft.

$$\begin{array}{r} 4 \text{ R2} \\ 3\overline{)14} \\ -12 \\ \hline 2 \end{array}$$

40 in. = _____ ft. _____ in.

52 ft. = _____ yd. _____ ft.

93 in. = _____ ft. _____ in.

Let's Learn!

You can measure the weight of an object using **customary units of weight**. This table shows the relationships between these units.

Customary units of weight
1 pound (lb.) = 16 ounces (oz.)
1 ton = 2,000 lb.

Convert each measurement.

2 lb. = __32__ oz.

$2 \times 16 = 32$

64 oz. = _____ lb.

6,000 lb. = _____ tons

20 oz. = _____ lb. _____ oz.

4 tons = _____ lb.

3,675 lb. = _____ ton _____ lb.

14 lb. = _____ oz.

35 oz. = _____ lb. _____ oz.

$\frac{1}{2}$ ton = _____ lb.

$5\frac{1}{2}$ lb. = _____ oz.

IXL.com
skill ID
XST

Draw a line between equivalent measurements.

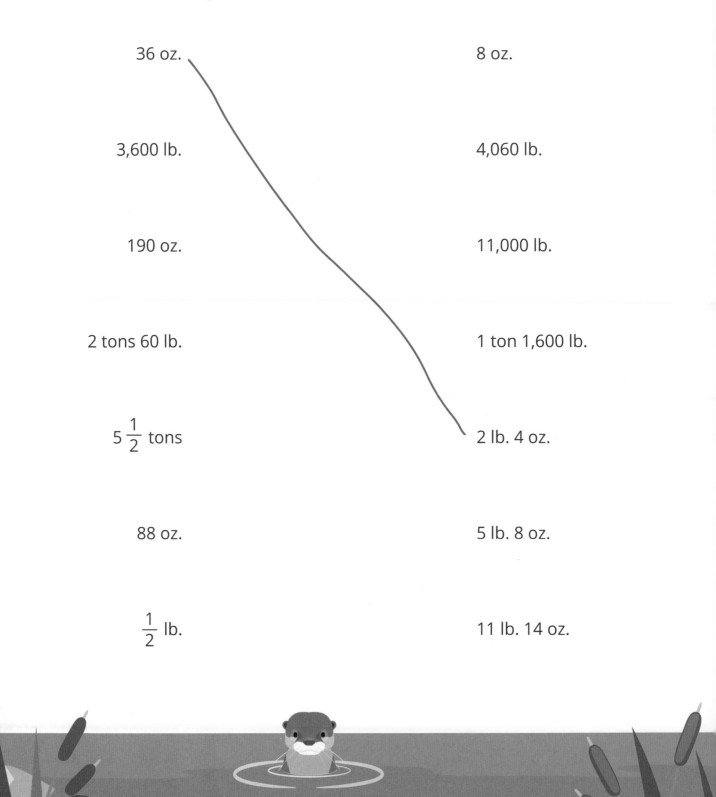

36 oz.	8 oz.
3,600 lb.	4,060 lb.
190 oz.	11,000 lb.
2 tons 60 lb.	1 ton 1,600 lb.
$5\frac{1}{2}$ tons	2 lb. 4 oz.
88 oz.	5 lb. 8 oz.
$\frac{1}{2}$ lb.	11 lb. 14 oz.

Let's Learn!

Capacity is used to measure the amount of liquid a container can hold. Look at the table to see some of the **customary units of capacity** and the relationships between them.

Customary units of capacity
1 cup (c.) = 8 fluid ounces (fl. oz.)
1 pint (pt.) = 2 c.
1 quart (qt.) = 2 pt.
1 gallon (gal.) = 4 qt.

Convert each measurement.

16 c. = ___8___ pt.

$16 \div 2 = 8$

4 c. = _____ fl. oz.

6 qt. = _____ gal. _____ qt.

5 gal. = _____ qt.

15 pt. = _____ qt. _____ pt.

27 fl. oz. = _____ c. _____ fl. oz.

$3 \frac{1}{2}$ qt. = _____ pt.

$10 \frac{1}{4}$ c. = _____ fl. oz.

27 qt. = _____ gal. _____ qt.

IXL.com
skill ID
96B

Convert each measurement.

144 fl. oz. = _____ c.   26 pt. = _____ c.

$5\frac{1}{4}$ gal. = _____ qt.   33 pt. = _____ qt. _____ pt.

Challenge yourself! Convert each measurement.

48 fl. oz. = ___6___ c. = ___3___ pt.

$48 \div 8 = 6 \qquad 6 \div 2 = 3$

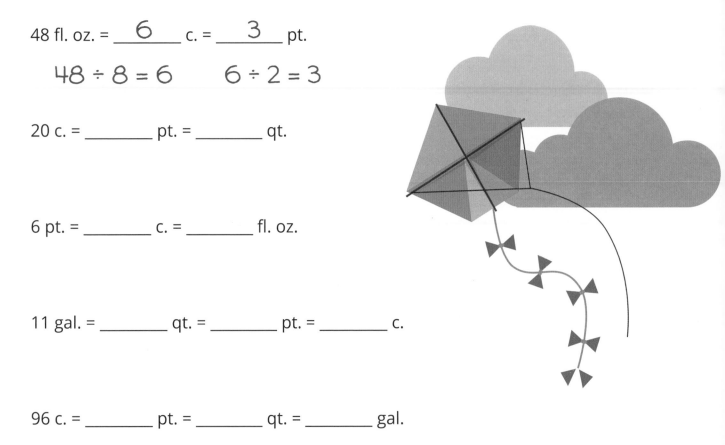

20 c. = _____ pt. = _____ qt.

6 pt. = _____ c. = _____ fl. oz.

11 gal. = _____ qt. = _____ pt. = _____ c.

96 c. = _____ pt. = _____ qt. = _____ gal.

THINK ABOUT IT! If you want to convert cups to gallons in one step, what number would you divide by?

Answer each question.

Ms. Jensen is throwing a birthday party for her daughter. She buys a roll of wrapping paper that is 15 feet long. How many **yards** of wrapping paper does she have?

_____

She buys 3 quarts of fruit punch to serve at the party. How many **cups** of fruit punch is that?

_____

She wants to make a photo booth for the party guests. She finds a backdrop that is 96 inches tall. What is the height of the backdrop, in **feet**?

_____

For the balloon decorations on the tables, Ms. Jensen buys a box of balloon weights. The box of weights is 192 ounces. How many **pounds** is that?

_____

IXL.com
skill ID
8DZ

Circle the best estimate for the measurement of each object.

Capacity of a juice box

180 milliliters   180 liters

Length of an eraser

12 millimeters   12 meters

Mass of a zebra

385 milligrams   385 kilograms

Length of a fishing pole

3 centimeters   3 meters

Circle the object that best matches the measurement.

5 kilograms

Mass of a bouncy ball

Mass of a bowling ball

14 centimeters

Length of a fork

Length of a car

2 meters

Length of a paper clip

Length of a bed

150 liters

Capacity of a bathtub

Capacity of a dog bowl

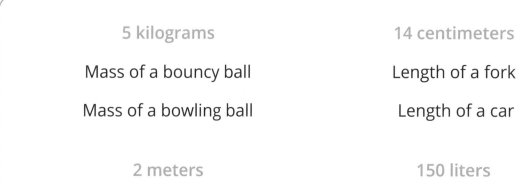

IXL.com
skill ID
S9U

Metric units of length

Let's Learn!

You can also measure lengths using **metric units of length**. This table shows the relationships between these units.

Metric units of length
1 centimeter (cm) = 10 millimeters (mm)
1 meter (m) = 100 cm
1 kilometer (km) = 1,000 m

You can use these relationships to convert between metric units. Sometimes, your answer will be a decimal. Try converting 1,560 meters to kilometers.

1,560 meters ÷ 1,000 meters per kilometer = 1.56 kilometers

Convert each measurement.

2.2 m = ___220___ cm

2.2 × 100 = 220

19 mm = _____ cm

45 cm = _____ mm

6.4 km = _____ m

253 cm = _____ m

8.43 cm = _____ mm

IXL.com
skill ID
8MZ

Find the path from start to finish! Move in the direction of the equivalent measurement. Continue until you reach the end.

START ↓

3 km	300 m	**8.1 m**	810 cm	**811 mm**
3,000 m		81 cm		81.1 cm
74 mm	7.4 cm	**5.4 m**	0.54 km	**6.05 cm**
0.74 cm		540 cm		60.5 mm
15,000 m	1.5 km	**3,570 m**	357 km	**74.2 km**
15 km		3.57 km		74,200 m
12.5 mm	1.25 cm	**436 mm**	43.6 cm	**FINISH**

Let's Learn!

The amount of matter in an object is called its **mass**, which is similar to its weight. You can measure mass using **metric units of mass**. This table shows the relationships between these units.

Metric units of mass
1 gram (g) = 1,000 milligrams (mg)
1 kilogram (kg) = 1,000 g

Convert each measurement.

8,400 mg = ____8.4____ g

$$8{,}400 \div 1{,}000 = 8.4$$

3 kg = _____ g

7,100 g = _____ kg

9,750 mg = _____ g

1.2 kg = _____ g

50,000 g = _____ kg

24,300 mg = _____ g

3.3 g = _____ mg

15,770 g = _____ kg

CHALLENGE ZONE

Fill in the blanks. Use each measurement once.

2.5 kg   25 g   2,500 mg

25,000 mg = _____ 25 G _____

2,500 g = _____ 2.5 KG _____

2.5 g = _____ 2,500 MG _____

3.7 g   3,070 mg   3.7 kg

3,700 mg = _____

3,700 g = _____

3.07 g = _____

12,400 mg   12.4 kg   1,240 mg

12,400 g = _____

12.4 g = _____

1.24 g = _____

5.1 g   51 g   51 kg

5,100 mg = _____

51,000 g = _____

51,000 mg = _____

1.89 kg   18,900 g   1,890 mg

1,890 g = _____

1.89 g = _____

18.9 kg = _____

6.5 g   0.65 kg   65 kg

65,000 g = _____

6,500 mg = _____

650 g = _____

You can also measure capacity using metric units. This table shows the relationship between two of the **metric units of capacity.**

Metric units of capacity
1 liter (L) = 1,000 milliliters (mL)

Convert each measurement.

9,400 mL = _____9.4_____ L

$$9,400 \div 1,000 = 9.4$$

8.3 L = _____ mL

6.02 L = _____ mL

310 mL = _____ L

1,700 mL = _____ L

15.6 L = _____ mL

2.41 L = _____ mL

45,200 mL = _____ L

3,840 mL = _____ L

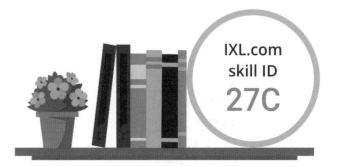

IXL.com
skill ID
27C

Circle the greater measurement in each pair.

| 3,400 mL | (3.42 L) | | 2.8 L | 20,800 mL |

| 56,000 mL | 5.06 L | | 1,400 mL | 10.4 L |

| 18,810 mL | 188.1 L | | 260 L | 26 mL |

| 77.7 L | 700,000 mL | | 128 mL | 1.28 L |

| 550 mL | 5.5 L | | 11 L | 11,100 mL |

Time to review! Compare the measurements using >, <, or =.

7,200 mg	<	720 g	7.3 cm	◯	73 mm
6,460 mL	◯	6.4 L	30 g	◯	3,000 mg
14,600 mg	◯	1.46 g	2.2 L	◯	2,200 mL
3,320 cm	◯	3.32 m	31.36 cm	◯	313 mm
805 mg	◯	80.5 g	52.2 km	◯	5,522 m

IXL.com
skill ID
2Q8

Answer each question.

Evelyn went to Toys and Games Galore with her family. She found a unicorn water bottle that holds 0.35 liters of water. How many **milliliters** of water can this bottle hold?

_____

Her brother wanted the Rip-Roaring Roller Coaster Model. The package says that the model will be 90 centimeters tall when fully built! How tall will it be in **millimeters**?

_____

Evelyn's sister found the Create-A-Beach Sand Kit. The kit comes with 1.2 kilograms of sand. How many **grams** of sand are in the kit?

_____

Her dad wanted to buy more bubbles for their bubble machine. Pop's Bubbles has 1.39 liters in a bottle. Super Sparkle Bubbles has 1,330 milliliters in a bottle. Which bottle has more?

_____

Add or subtract. Regroup your answer, if necessary.

2 hours 38 minutes + 3 hours 45 minutes = ___6 HOURS 23 MINUTES___

4 hours 56 minutes − 2 hours 12 minutes = _____

2 hours 19 minutes + 2 hours 40 minutes = _____

3 hours 31 minutes − 1 hour 36 minutes = _____

3 hours 27 minutes − 29 minutes = _____

2 hours 38 minutes + 1 hour 50 minutes = _____

1 hour 48 minutes + 14 minutes = _____

Write the amount of time that has passed between each starting time and ending time.

1 HOUR 36 MINUTES

Write each missing starting or ending time based on the time passed.

__12:55 P.M.__   2 hours 39 minutes

_____   2 hours 15 minutes

_____   4 hours 27 minutes

_____   4 hours 45 minutes

_____   6 hours 44 minutes

Answer each question.

Noah and Abigail spent the day at the Science and Technology Museum. Before they arrived, they made a list of everything they wanted to do there.

STATIONS
FOSSIL ADVENTURES	ROBOTICS
3-D PRINTING	BEEHIVE PROJECT

SHOWS
BIRDS IN NATURE (9:45 A.M.)

CHEMISTRY MAGIC (1:30 P.M.)

They first went to the Birds in Nature show. The show lasted 35 minutes. How much time did they have until the Chemistry Magic show began?

_____

Next they went to the stations. They started at Fossil Adventures at 10:27 a.m., and they finished at the Beehive Project at 1:04 p.m. How long did they spend at the stations?

_____

They left the museum at 2:34 p.m. If they were at the museum for 5 hours and 13 minutes, when did they arrive?

_____

Let's Learn!

A **polygon** is a closed figure whose sides are all straight lines.

This shape is a **polygon**.
Its sides are straight and connected.

This shape is **not a polygon**.
It has a curved edge, and it is not closed.

Circle the polygons.

KEEP IT GOING! | Can you draw another polygon that is not on this page?

IXL.com
skill ID
ZH6

Let's Learn!

You can name a polygon by its number of sides. Look at the examples below.

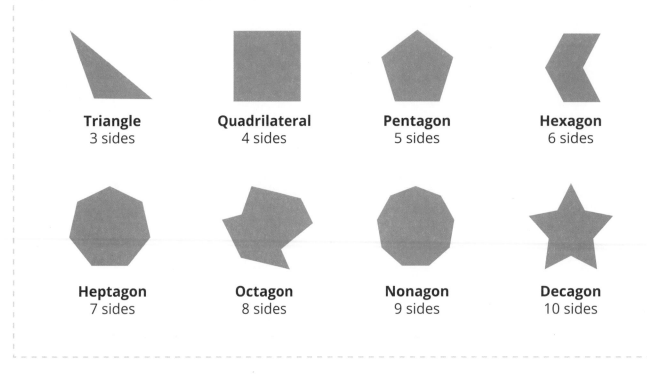

Triangle
3 sides

Quadrilateral
4 sides

Pentagon
5 sides

Hexagon
6 sides

Heptagon
7 sides

Octagon
8 sides

Nonagon
9 sides

Decagon
10 sides

Name each polygon.

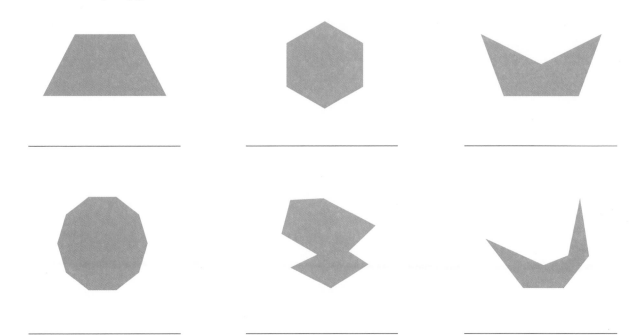

If a polygon has equal side lengths and equal angle measures, it is a **regular polygon**.

This is a **regular polygon**. All of its sides are equal, and all of its angles are equal.

This is an **irregular polygon**. It has different side lengths and different angle measures.

Circle the figures that are regular polygons.

IXL.com
skill ID
UHC

Let's Learn!

You can classify angles by their measure. Here are four types of angles: **acute**, **right**, **obtuse**, and **straight**.

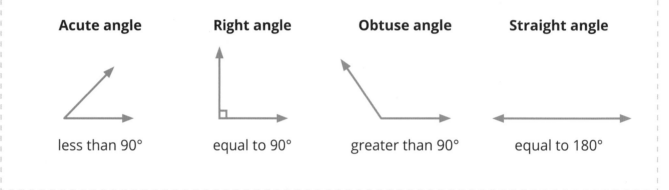

Acute angle	Right angle	Obtuse angle	Straight angle
less than 90°	equal to 90°	greater than 90°	equal to 180°

Classify each angle as acute, right, obtuse, or straight.

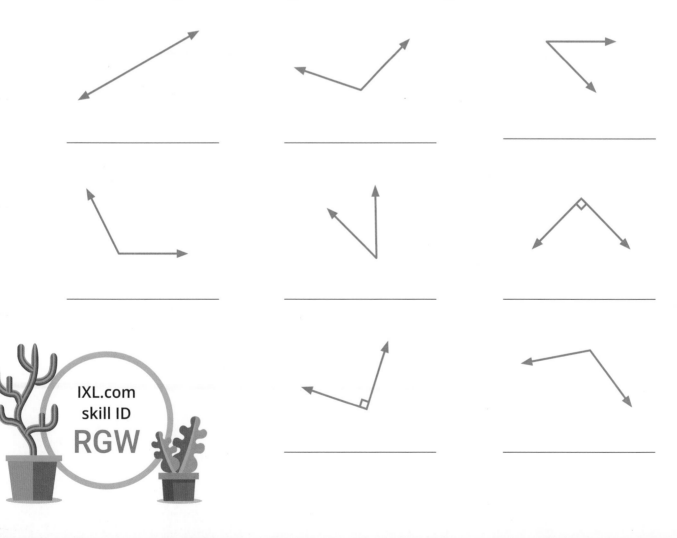

IXL.com
skill ID
RGW

Parallel lines are lines that never cross. **Perpendicular lines** are lines that form a 90° angle.

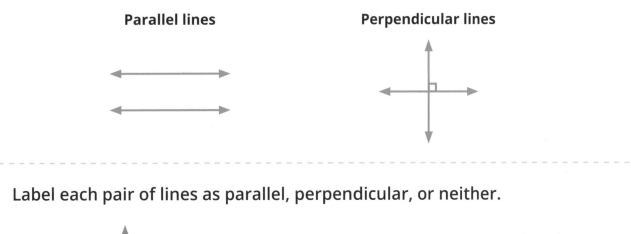

Label each pair of lines as parallel, perpendicular, or neither.

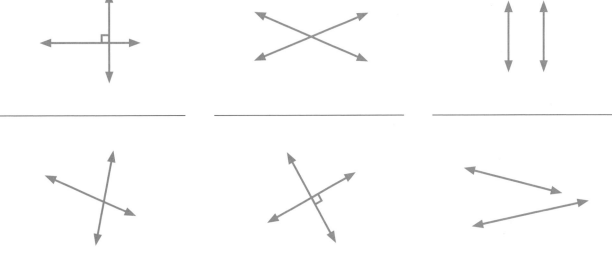

_____   _____   _____

_____   _____   _____

Let's Learn!

You can classify triangles by their angle measures. The three types are **acute**, **right**, and **obtuse**.

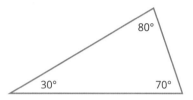 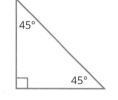 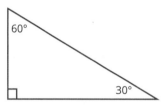

A triangle is **acute** if all three angles are less than 90°.

A triangle is **right** if one of its angles is 90°.

A triangle is **obtuse** if one of its angles is greater than 90°.

Classify each triangle by its angle measures.

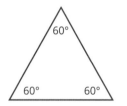 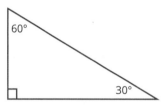 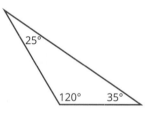

ACUTE _____ _____

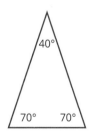 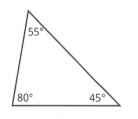 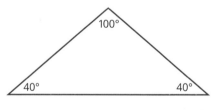

_____ _____ _____

IXL.com
skill ID
N77

Let's Learn!

You can also classify triangles by their side lengths. Triangles can be **equilateral**, **isosceles**, or **scalene**. You can use markings to show equal side lengths.

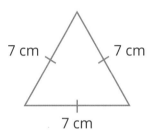

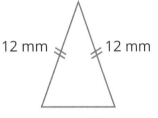

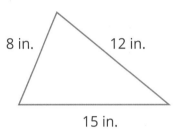

A triangle is **equilateral** if all 3 side lengths are equal.

A triangle is **isosceles** if two of its side lengths are equal.

A triangle is **scalene** if none of its side lengths are equal.

Classify each triangle by its side lengths.

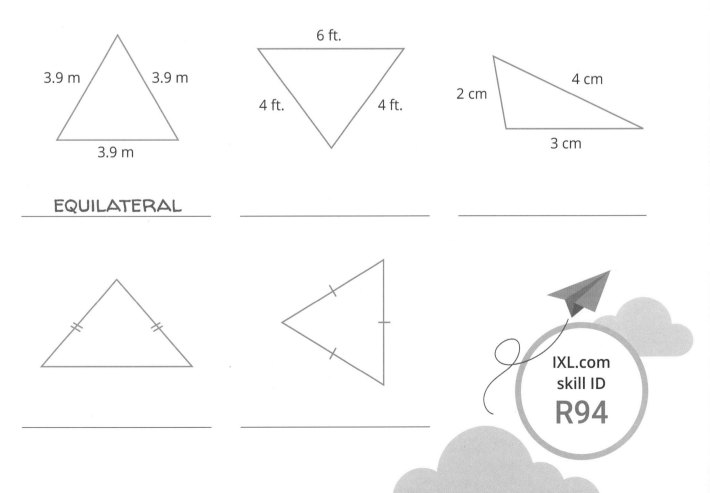

EQUILATERAL

IXL.com
skill ID
R94

Let's Learn!

Quadrilaterals are polygons with exactly four sides. Look at the examples below to see different types of quadrilaterals. As with sides, you can use markings to show equal angles.

A **parallelogram** is a quadrilateral with two pairs of parallel sides.

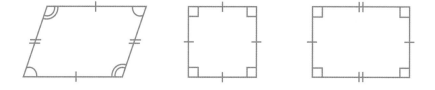

A **rectangle** is a parallelogram with four right angles.

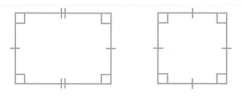

A **rhombus** is a parallelogram with four equal side lengths.

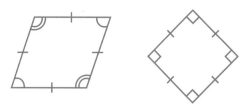

A **square** is a parallelogram with four equal side lengths and four right angles. So, a square can also be called a rectangle and a rhombus.

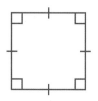

A **trapezoid** is a quadrilateral with only one pair of parallel sides.

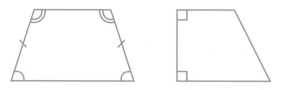

Quadrilaterals

Write the shape names to complete the graphic organizer.

Word bank		
parallelogram	rhombus	rectangle
square	trapezoid	quadrilateral

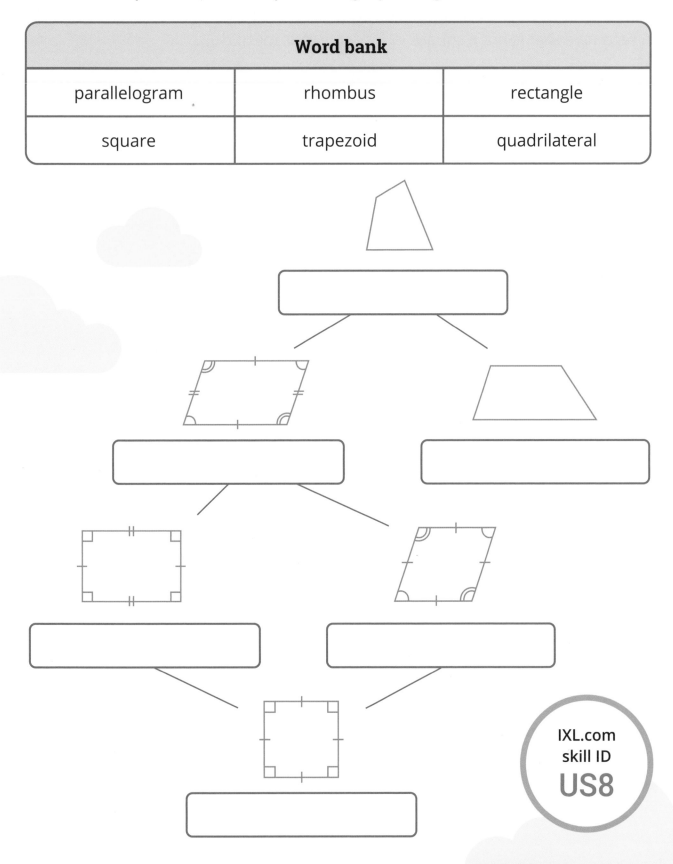

IXL.com
skill ID
US8

Draw each shape. Try not to draw the same shape twice!

A rectangle that is not a square

A trapezoid

A quadrilateral that is not a trapezoid

A parallelogram that is not a rectangle

A rhombus

A quadrilateral that is not a parallelogram

Let's Learn!

Polyhedrons are three-dimensional figures made of all flat surfaces. Each flat surface is called a **face**. The faces meet to form **edges**. All of the faces are polygons, and their corners are called **vertices**.

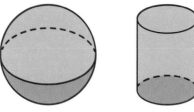

These figures are polyhedrons.
They are made up of flat surfaces.

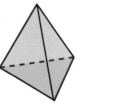 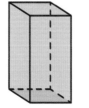

These figures are **not** polyhedrons.
They have curved surfaces.

Circle all of the polyhedrons.

 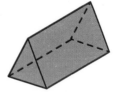 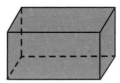

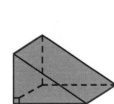 

Let's Learn!

Two special types of polyhedrons are called **prisms** and **pyramids**. Prisms have two parallel **bases** connected by rectangular faces. Pyramids have one **base** and triangular faces that meet at a point.

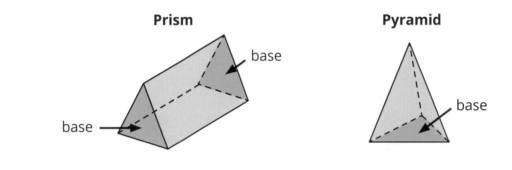

Prism

base

base

Pyramid

base

Determine whether each figure is a prism, a pyramid, or neither.

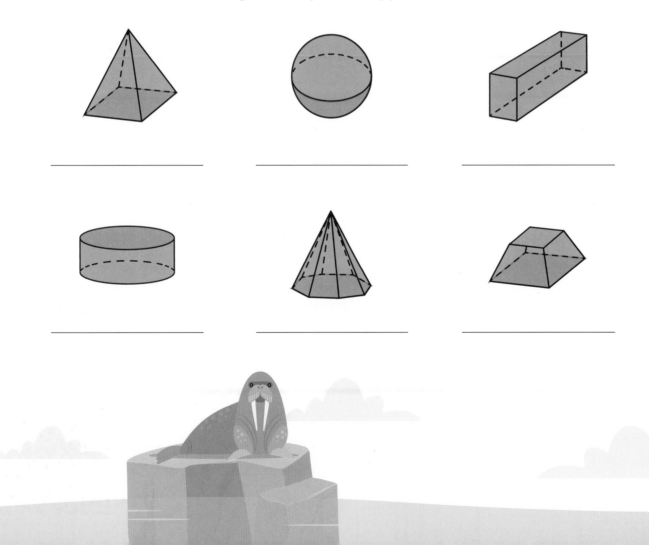

_____   _____   _____

_____   _____   _____

Find the perimeter of each shape. Simplify your answers.

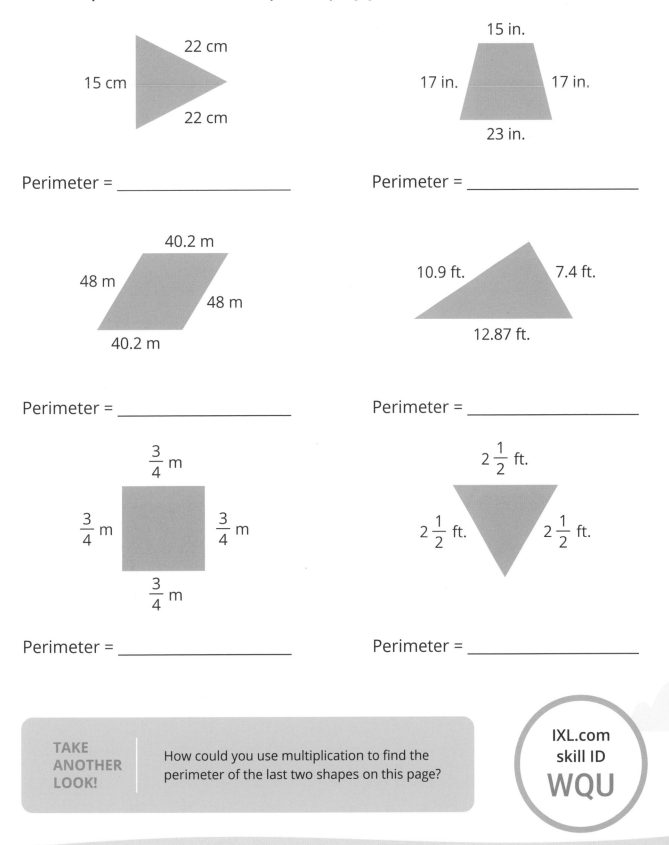

22 cm

15 cm

22 cm

Perimeter = _____

15 in.

17 in.   17 in.

23 in.

Perimeter = _____

40.2 m

48 m

48 m

40.2 m

Perimeter = _____

10.9 ft.   7.4 ft.

12.87 ft.

Perimeter = _____

$\frac{3}{4}$ m

$\frac{3}{4}$ m $\frac{3}{4}$ m

$\frac{3}{4}$ m

Perimeter = _____

$2\frac{1}{2}$ ft.

$2\frac{1}{2}$ ft. $2\frac{1}{2}$ ft.

Perimeter = _____

TAKE ANOTHER LOOK! How could you use multiplication to find the perimeter of the last two shapes on this page?

IXL.com
skill ID
WQU

Find the area of each shape. Simplify your answers.

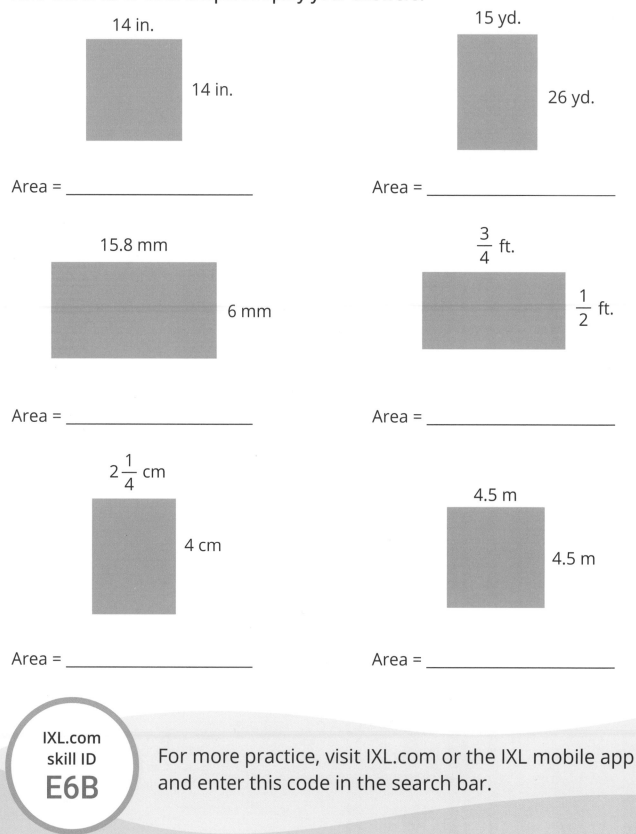

14 in.

14 in.

Area = _____

15 yd.

26 yd.

Area = _____

15.8 mm

6 mm

Area = _____

$\frac{3}{4}$ ft.

$\frac{1}{2}$ ft.

Area = _____

$2\frac{1}{4}$ cm

4 cm

Area = _____

4.5 m

4.5 m

Area = _____

Use the perimeter to find the missing side length.

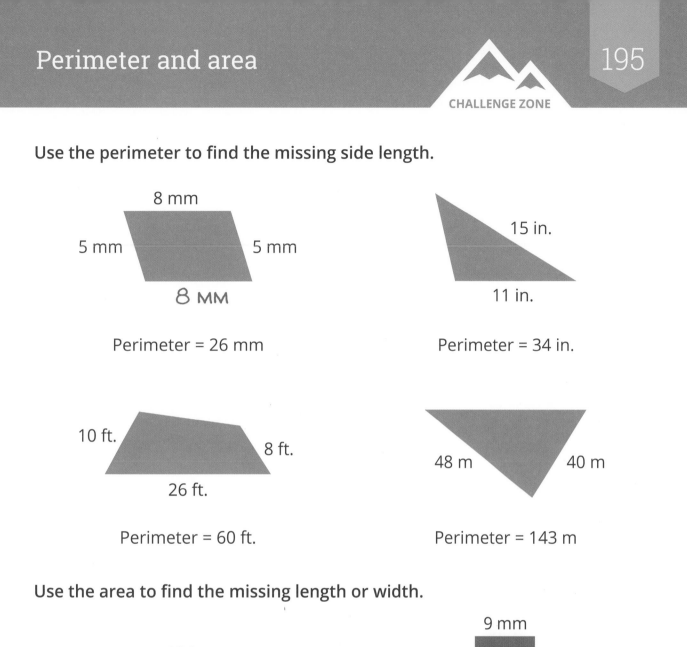

8 mm

5 mm   5 mm

8 MM

Perimeter = 26 mm

15 in.

11 in.

Perimeter = 34 in.

10 ft.

8 ft.

26 ft.

Perimeter = 60 ft.

48 m   40 m

Perimeter = 143 m

Use the area to find the missing length or width.

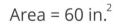

12 in.

Area = 60 in.^{2}

9 mm

Area = 171 mm^2

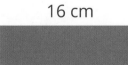

16 cm

Area = 112 cm^2

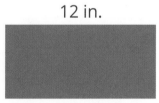

Answer each question.

Patrick has a rectangular picnic blanket that is 59 inches wide and 76 inches long. What is the area of his blanket?

_____

An artist is making an oil painting to hang in his studio. He is using a square canvas with side lengths of 24 inches. What is the area of this canvas?

_____

Molly wants to build a fence around her yard for her puppy. She has a rectangular yard that is 75 feet wide and 82 feet long. What is the perimeter of her yard?

_____

Jessica made a decorative case for a pillow. The pillowcase was 27.6 inches long and 15.7 inches wide, and she sewed a border around the edges. What was the total length of the border?

_____

The owner of Hole-in-One Donuts is making a large, rectangular banner for the store's grand opening. The area of the banner is 54 square feet. If the width of the banner is 3 feet, what is its length?

_____

Let's Learn!

The amount of space inside a three-dimensional figure is called its **volume**. To find volume, you can count the number of **unit cubes** in a figure. A unit cube has edge lengths of 1 unit and a volume of 1 cubic unit.

unit cube

Try finding the volume of the figure below.

There are 3 layers of cubes in this prism.

Each layer has 2 × 4 = 8 cubes.

4 cubes

2 cubes

8 cubes × 3 layers = 24 cubes

Since there are 24 unit cubes, the volume of the prism can be written as 24 cubic units. You can also write the volume as 24 units^3.

Find the volume of each figure.

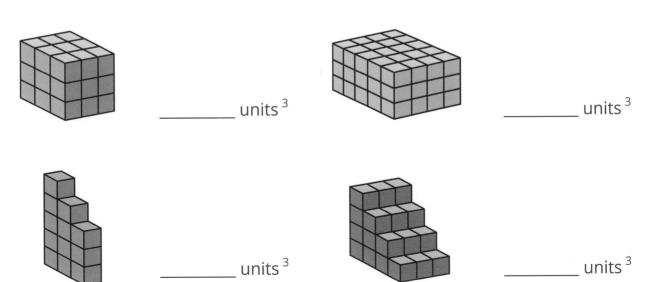

_____ units^3

_____ units^3

_____ units^3

_____ units^3

Let's Learn!

You can find the volume of a rectangular prism by multiplying its length, width, and height! Look at the unit cubes to understand why this is true.

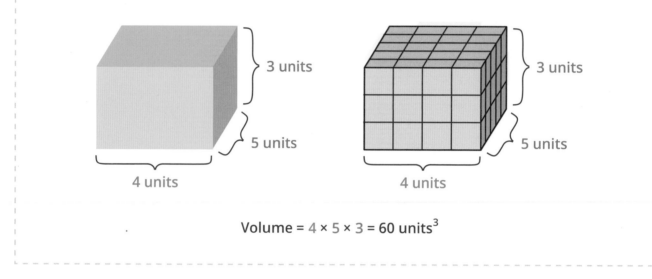

3 units

5 units

4 units

3 units

5 units

4 units

Volume = 4 × 5 × 3 = 60 units^3

Find the volume of each prism.

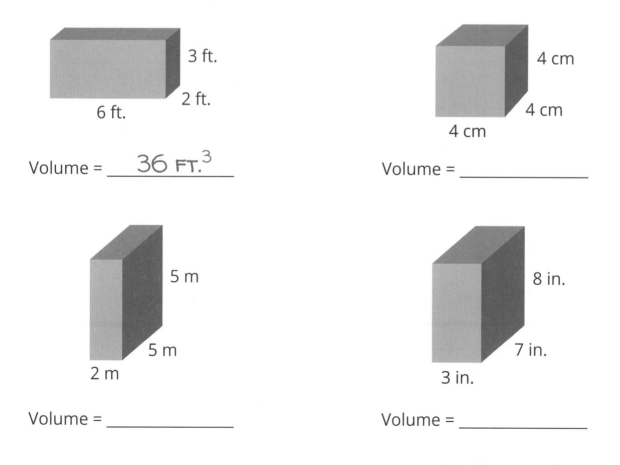

3 ft.

2 ft.

6 ft.

Volume = ___36 FT.^{3}___

4 cm

4 cm

4 cm

Volume = _____

5 m

5 m

2 m

Volume = _____

8 in.

7 in.

3 in.

Volume = _____

Find the volume of each prism. Simplify your answers.

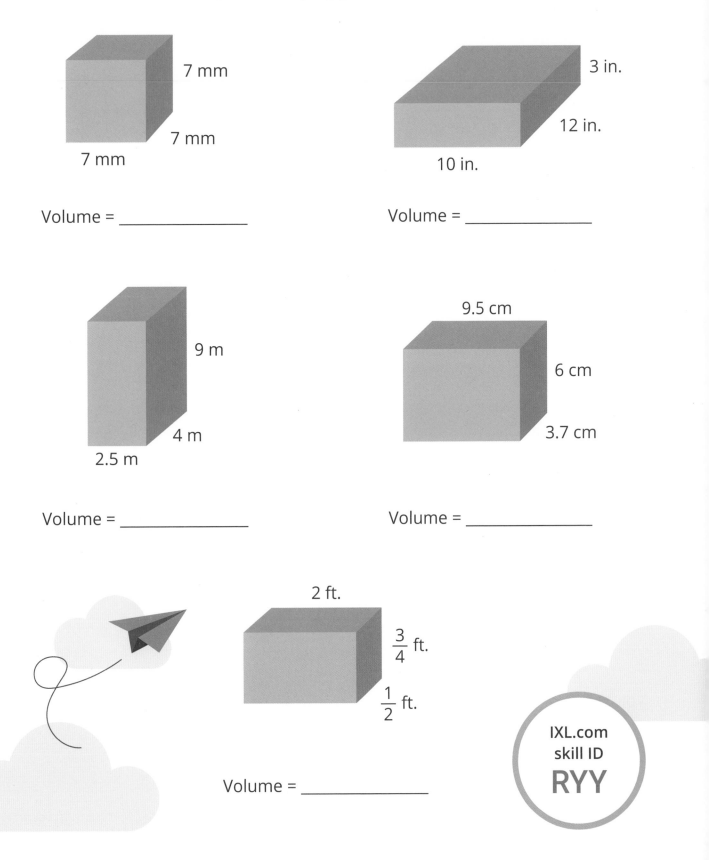

7 mm

7 mm

7 mm

Volume = _____

3 in.

12 in.

10 in.

Volume = _____

9 m

4 m

2.5 m

Volume = _____

9.5 cm

6 cm

3.7 cm

Volume = _____

2 ft.

$\frac{3}{4}$ ft.

$\frac{1}{2}$ ft.

Volume = _____

Let's Learn!

Composite figures are figures that are made of more than one shape. You can find the volume of composite figures by breaking them into smaller figures. Try it with the figure below!

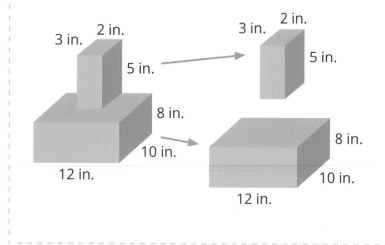

Find the volume of the top prism.
$3 \times 2 \times 5 = 30$ in.^{3}

Find the volume of the bottom prism.
$12 \times 10 \times 8 = 960$ in.^{3}

Then, add the two volumes together.
30 in.$^3 + 960$ in.$^3 = 990$ in.^{3}

Find the volume of each figure.

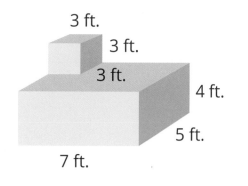

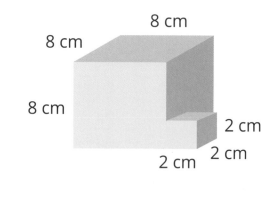

Volume = _____

Volume = _____

Keep going! Find the volume of each figure.

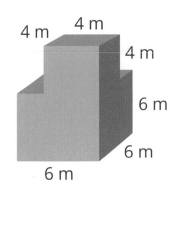

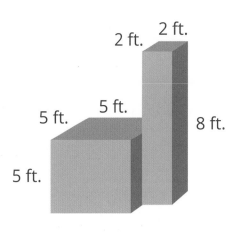

Volume = _____

Volume = _____

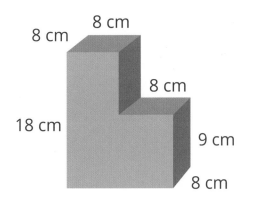

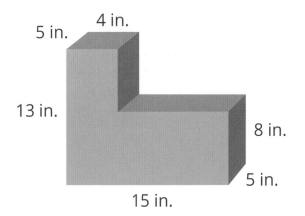

Volume = _____

Volume = _____

Answer each question. Simplify your answers.

Allison is making her favorite chicken chili recipe. Here are the ingredients she needs.

Chicken Chili Recipe

INGREDIENTS:

Two 15 oz. cans of black beans

Two 15 oz. cans of white beans

Two 14.5 oz. cans of diced tomatoes

2 cups heavy cream

$\frac{1}{2}$ cup diced onion

One and a half 10 oz. packages of frozen chopped spinach

2 tablespoons butter

$1\frac{1}{2}$ teaspoon salt

2 tablespoons chili powder

$3\frac{1}{2}$ cups chicken broth

2 chicken breasts

$1\frac{1}{4}$ teaspoon oregano

How many total ounces of diced tomatoes does Allison need? _____

How much more salt than oregano does she need? _____

She has a 4-cup box of chicken broth. How much chicken broth will she have left over after making the chili? _____

Allison wants her chili to have a mild flavor. She decides to use $\frac{1}{4}$ the amount of chili powder shown in the recipe. How many tablespoons of chili powder will she use? _____

Answer each question. Simplify your answers.

Allison loves spinach, so she doubles the amount of chopped spinach in the recipe. How many ounces of chopped spinach will she use?

_____

Allison buys the chicken breasts at the grocery store. The package that she buys weighs 2.5 pounds total. If the chicken breasts are about the same size, how much does each one weigh?

_____

She also buys a 1-quart container of heavy cream. How many **cups** of heavy cream will she have left after making the chili?

_____

She starts making the chili by combining the salt and oregano in a small bowl. How many teaspoons is that in all?

_____

Allison uses a $\frac{1}{3}$-cup measuring cup for the heavy cream. How many times will she need to fill the measuring cup to measure out all of the cream?

_____

IXL.com
skill ID
W9K

Answer each question.

Grove Town is opening a new community center. The community center will be open from 7:45 a.m. to 8 p.m. on weekdays. How long will the center be open each weekday?

_____

The center will offer 20 fitness classes each week. Of the fitness classes, $\frac{1}{4}$ will be water aerobics classes. How many water aerobics classes will there be each week?

_____

The center will also hold a summer camp this year. There are 126 children signed up for the camp. If the campers will be split into 14 different groups, how many campers will be in each group?

_____

Grove Town
Community Center

Answer each question.

The community center will have two computer labs. The first lab will have 3 rows of computers with 4 in each row. The second lab will have 5 rows with 3 computers in each row. Write an expression for the total number of computers at the community center.

_____

Builders are installing the new floor for the gymnasium. The floor will be 60 feet long and 38 feet wide. What is the area of the new gymnasium floor?

_____

The center will also have an outdoor basketball court. There will be 4 basketball hoops, and each one costs $852.50. What is the total cost of the basketball hoops?

_____

The center plans to have a community garden with a fence around the perimeter. If the garden will be 32.5 feet wide and 48 feet long, how many feet of fencing will be needed?

_____

IXL.com
skill ID
7SX

Answer each question.

Joanne's Antiques sells many different items. At the front of the store, there is an antique wooden desk that costs $1,724. On top of the desk is a gold lamp. The desk costs exactly 10 times as much as the lamp. How much does the lamp cost?

_____

A customer buys a tea set that costs $87.79. If she pays with a $100 bill, how much change will she receive?

_____

Another customer is looking at the Persian rugs. Each rug is 9.5 feet wide and 12 feet long. What is the area of each rug?

_____

The rugs are on sale for $2,355 each. How much would 3 rugs cost?

_____

Joanne's Antiques also sells ornaments. There are 36 ornaments, and $\frac{1}{3}$ of them are made of glass. How many ornaments are made of glass?

_____

IXL.com
skill ID
APD

Answer each question.

Matt works at Joanne's Antiques, and he earns $11.25 per hour. How much will he earn if he works 8 hours?

_____

Matt helps organize the jewelry in the new countertop display. The rectangular display case is 15 inches long, 8 inches wide, and 3 inches tall. What is the volume of this display case?

_____

Joanne's Antiques received a few vintage tablecloths this week. One tablecloth is 2 yards long. How long is that tablecloth, in **feet**?

_____

The store also bought a set of 6 antique chairs. If the chairs cost $2,055 total, what was the price of each chair?

_____

Answer each question.

The Greenville High School track team went to the state championship last weekend. Gabriella and Hailey both ran the 100-meter dash for the team. Gabriella ran the race in 12.24 seconds. Hailey ran it in 13.78 seconds. How much faster was Gabriella's time?

_____

Sadie and 3 of her teammates ran a relay race. Each person ran an equal part of the race. If each person ran 800 meters, what was the total distance they ran, in **kilometers**?

_____

Carter arrived at the track meet at 11:47 a.m. His race started at 3:35 p.m. How much time did he have between his arrival and his race?

_____

Before his race, Brandon ran $\frac{1}{2}$ of a mile to warm up. Then, he ran the 2-mile race. How many total **yards** did Brandon run?

_____

The shot-put event happened every 20 minutes from 3:40 p.m. to 5:20 p.m. What were all the times of the shot-put event?

_____

IXL.com
skill ID
MJ9

Answer each question.

Jayden competed in the high jump for the team. He jumped over a bar that was $6\frac{1}{4}$ feet high. How many **inches** high was the bar?

_____

Jayden's parents came to watch his event. They paid a total of $10.00 for their tickets. They also bought 2 orders of popcorn at the concession stand for $4.99 each. How much did they spend in all?

_____

Claire competed in both the high jump and the long jump. Use the coordinate plane below to write the ordered pair of the high-jump event.

_____

If Claire walked from the high jump to the long jump, how far did she walk, in units?

_____

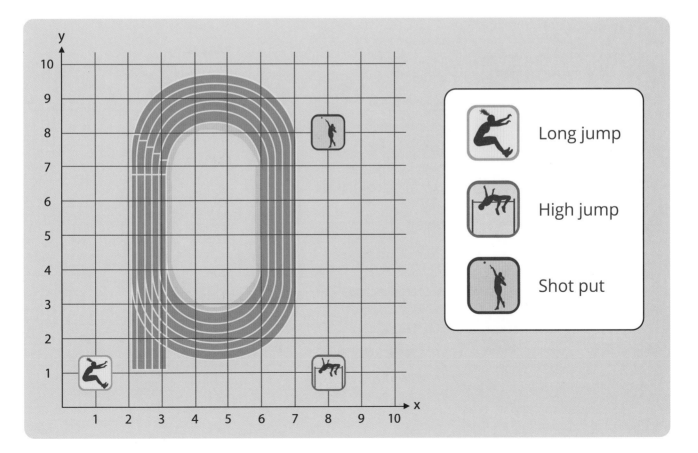

PAGE 2

⑤,448   3,48①,966
2③,481   17⑧,931

2②8,384   6,4⑧4,281
2,2③4,725   ④8,276

7,②85,395   ⑨48,285
①64,481   2,⑤28,947

PAGE 3

5,945
70,325
676,080
490,529
305,173
2,050,708

50,000 + 6,000 + 700 + 10
200,000 + 60,000 + 10 + 7
100,000 + 80,000 + 4,000 + 5
4,000,000 + 90,000 + 5,000 + 800
9,000,000 + 500,000 + 60,000

PAGE 4

3,504 — three thousand five hundred four

222,000 — two hundred twenty-two thousand

6,050,000 — six million fifty thousand

950,003 — nine hundred fifty thousand three

70,020 — seventy thousand twenty

3,000,504 — three million five hundred four

6,500,000 — six million five hundred thousand

2,022,000 — two million twenty-two thousand

7,200 — seven thousand two hundred

9,503 — nine thousand five hundred three

PAGE 5

80,000 is 10 times as much as 8,000.
400 is 10 times as much as 40.
5,000 is 10 times as much as 500.
2,000,000 is 10 times as much as 200,000.
70 is 10 times as much as 7.
300,000 is 10 times as much as 30,000.

PAGE 6

7,171 < 7,711   53,385 > 5,385
2,473 < 23,474   1,618 < 16,180
67,817 > 67,717   59,926 < 599,926
613,240 > 61,324   1,221,122 > 1,121,122
750,004 > 570,004   3,444,924 < 3,444,927
100,001 < 100,010   9,005,757 < 9,500,700

PAGE 7

7,148   7,418   7,841
40,884   41,884   44,480
6,893   68,963   686,933
552,777   557,727   575,727
4,988,919 4,988,991 4,989,119

PAGE 8

9 × 400 = 3,600
40 × 80 = 3,200

20 × 90 = 1,800
3 × 500 = 1,500

6 × 400 = 2,400
30 × 200 = 6,000

3 × 6,000 = 18,000
2 × 7,000 = 14,000

2 × 80,000 = 160,000
600 × 70 = 42,000

PAGE 9

50 × 500 = 25,000
700 × 10 = 7,000

6 × 60,000 = 360,000
300 × 800 = 240,000

800 × 700 = 560,000
5 × 11,000 = 55,000

4 × 20,000 = 80,000
9 × 10,000 = 90,000

PAGE 9, continued

300 × 1,000 = 300,000
7 × 300,000 = 2,100,000

9 × 70,000 = 630,000
400 × 5,000 = 2,000,000

8 × 8,000,000 = 64,000,000
9,000 × 600 = 5,400,000

5,000 × 800 = 4,000,000
90 × 800,000 = 72,000,000

PAGE 10

22 × 38 is about 20 × 40 = 800
31 × 33 is about 30 × 30 = 900
17 × 72 is about 20 × 70 = 1,400
88 × 42 is about 90 × 40 = 3,600
49 × 58 is about 50 × 60 = 3,000
62 × 29 is about 60 × 30 = 1,800
78 × 51 is about 80 × 50 = 4,000
89 × 79 is about 90 × 80 = 7,200

PAGE 11

4 × 82 = 328   7 × 34 = 238
8 × 56 = 448   3 × 96 = 288
2 × 87 = 174   5 × 41 = 205
6 × 79 = 474   9 × 68 = 612

PAGE 12

7 × 235 = 1,645   4 × 128 = 512
8 × 373 = 2,984   6 × 299 = 1,794
5 × 567 = 2,835   3 × 948 = 2,844
9 × 726 = 6,534   7 × 679 = 4,753

PAGE 13

37	29	145
× 4	× 6	× 5
148	174	725

381	726	808
× 9	× 3	× 2
3,429	2,178	1,616

577	639	984
× 8	× 7	× 9
4,616	4,473	8,856

1,058	3,450	1,783
× 3	× 4	× 6
3,174	13,800	10,698

PAGE 14

34	28	52
× 23	× 11	× 38
782	308	1,976

30	64	72
× 79	× 56	× 27
2,370	3,584	1,944

88	76	45
× 44	× 91	× 83
3,872	6,916	3,735

PAGE 15

112	368	454
× 23	× 14	× 32
2,576	5,152	14,528

509	719	346
× 47	× 22	× 56
23,923	15,818	19,376

595	738	827
× 58	× 63	× 85
34,510	46,494	70,295

642	434	763
× 79	× 94	× 88
50,718	40,796	67,144

PAGE 16

1,531	3,174	2,820
× 25	× 43	× 35
38,275	136,482	98,700

1,898	7,118	5,055
× 17	× 50	× 26
32,266	355,900	131,430

2,787	3,118	5,718
× 49	× 89	× 77
136,563	277,502	440,286

	4,510	9,628
	× 76	× 87
	342,760	837,636

PAGE 17

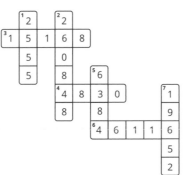

PAGE 18

1,472 < 1,591

2,842 = 2,842

16,467 > 14,112

120,198 < 120,432

PAGE 19

78 jars

384 muffins

2,470 miles

$2,136

99,425 pounds

PAGE 20

$1,398

2,496 miles

4,200 beads

6,426 pages

PAGE 21

18,000 ÷ 6 = 3,000

56,000 ÷ 80 = 700

48,000 ÷ 8 = 6,000

30,000 ÷ 6 = 5,000

2,700 ÷ 30 = 90

280,000 ÷ 7 = 40,000

500,000 ÷ 5 = 100,000

64,000 ÷ 80 = 800

350,000 ÷ 7 = 50,000

2,000 ÷ 50 = 40

490,000 ÷ 70 = 7,000

110,000 ÷ 11 = 10,000

PAGE 22

1,800,000 ÷ 9 = 200,000

3,200,000 ÷ 80 = 40,000

1,000,000 ÷ 10 = 100,000

4,800,000 ÷ 12 = 400,000

3,000,000 ÷ 5 = 600,000

140,000 ÷ 70 = 2,000

720,000 ÷ 60 = 12,000

600,000 ÷ 12 = 50,000

200,000 ÷ 20 = 10,000

8,100,000 ÷ 90 = 90,000

200,000 ÷ 40 = 5,000

4,000,000 ÷ 50 = 80,000

3,600,000 ÷ 40 = 90,000

PAGE 23

18 R2	24	13 R1
5)92	3)72	6)79

14	115	27
7)98	8)920	4)108

31 R4	48	35
7)221	6)288	9)315

112	203 R2	77 R8
8)896	4)814	9)701

Answers may vary. One possible answer is shown below.

You can multiply the divisor by the quotient and add the remainder to get the dividend.

For example, 9 × 77 + 8 = 701.

PAGE 24

315 R2	61	74
3)947	8)488	6)444

104	102 R4	256
9)936	7)718	5)1,280

403 R4	287	256
8)3,228	9)2,583	6)1,536

PAGE 25

737 ÷ 3 = 245 R2   912 ÷ 8 = 114

2,322 ÷ 6 = 387   2,209 ÷ 4 = 552 R1

Answer key

PAGE 26

46 bags

18 chairs

$435

They needed 24 lanes for all of the students. There were 4 students on the lane that was not full.

PAGE 27

158 ÷ 8 is close to 20.

263 ÷ 9 is close to 30.

368 ÷ 7 is close to 50.

104 ÷ 5 is close to 20.

371 ÷ 6 is close to 60.

651 ÷ 9 is close to 70.

719 ÷ 8 is close to 90.

355 ÷ 4 is close to 90.

PAGE 28

64 ÷ 31 is close to 2.

57 ÷ 29 is close to 2.

83 ÷ 41 is close to 2.

73 ÷ 18 is close to 4.

98 ÷ 19 is close to 5.

65 ÷ 22 is close to 3.

PAGE 29

638 ÷ 79 is close to 8.

551 ÷ 61 is close to 9.

253 ÷ 42 is close to 6.

368 ÷ 53 is close to 7.

111 ÷ 27 is close to 4.

442 ÷ 88 is close to 5.

PAGE 30

$$29\overline{)348} = 12 \qquad 22\overline{)475} = 21\,R13 \qquad 27\overline{)621} = 23$$

$$21\overline{)663} = 31\,R12 \qquad 31\overline{)682} = 22 \qquad 18\overline{)972} = 54$$

PAGE 31

$$46\overline{)552} = 12 \qquad 22\overline{)687} = 31\,R5 \qquad 19\overline{)574} = 30\,R4$$

$$21\overline{)882} = 42 \qquad 28\overline{)912} = 32\,R16 \qquad 82\overline{)904} = 11\,R2$$

PAGE 31, *continued*

$$35\overline{)779} = 22\,R9 \qquad 28\overline{)646} = 23\,R2 \qquad 13\overline{)1,456} = 112$$

$$17\overline{)2,414} = 142 \qquad 28\overline{)5,634} = 201\,R6$$

PAGE 32

$$31\overline{)254} = 8\,R6 \qquad 28\overline{)159} = 5\,R19 \qquad 31\overline{)218} = 7\,R1$$

$$29\overline{)174} = 6 \qquad 32\overline{)2,241} = 70\,R1 \qquad 27\overline{)1,701} = 63$$

PAGE 33

$$19\overline{)1,425} = 75 \qquad 32\overline{)1,314} = 41\,R2 \qquad 27\overline{)1,221} = 45\,R6$$

$$42\overline{)1,263} = 30\,R3 \qquad 17\overline{)1,001} = 58\,R15 \qquad 28\overline{)1,980} = 70\,R20$$

$$36\overline{)1,191} = 33\,R3 \qquad 38\overline{)3,116} = 82 \qquad 41\overline{)1,271} = 31$$

$$18\overline{)1,152} = 64 \qquad 53\overline{)1,601} = 30\,R11$$

PAGE 35

$$21\overline{)588} = 28 \qquad 17\overline{)153} = 9 \qquad 39\overline{)311} = 7\,R38$$

$$29\overline{)841} = 29 \qquad 64\overline{)530} = 8\,R18 \qquad 34\overline{)942} = 27\,R24$$

$$42\overline{)2,294} = 54\,R26 \qquad 58\overline{)2,262} = 39 \qquad 93\overline{)1,825} = 19\,R58$$

PAGE 36

$$43\overline{)818} = 19\,R1 \qquad 19\overline{)722} = 38 \qquad 46\overline{)414} = 9$$

$$31\overline{)1,922} = 62 \qquad 37\overline{)1,519} = 41\,R2 \qquad 84\overline{)3,870} = 46\,R6$$

$$29\overline{)2,639} = 91 \qquad 28\overline{)1,179} = 42\,R3 \qquad 34\overline{)1,033} = 30\,R13$$

PAGE 37

17 treasure boxes

24 fish

$16

There will be 19 full boxes and 8 glasses in the box that is not full.

PAGE 38

674 × 3 = 2,022

188 ÷ 5 = 37 R3

408 ÷ 6 = 68

4 × 1,259 = 5,036

2,116 ÷ 9 = 235 R1

88 × 17 = 1,496

36 × 52 = 1,872

674 ÷ 21 = 32 R2

PAGE 39

145 ÷ 18 = 8 R1

17 × 296 = 5,032

4,329 × 66 = 285,714

6,300 ÷ 28 = 225

5,547 × 79 = 438,213

8,558 ÷ 19 = 450 R8

7,106 ÷ 34 = 209

1,735 ÷ 36 = 48 R7

PAGE 40

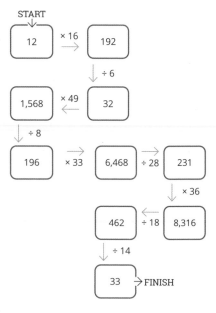

PAGE 41

$8 \times 8 \times 8 \times 8 \times 8 \times 8 \times 8 = 8^7$

$9 \times 9 \times 9 = 9^3$

$3 \times 3 \times 3 \times 3 \times 3 \times 3 = 3^6$

$10 \times 10 = 10^2$

$12 \times 12 = 12^2$

$78 \times 78 \times 78 \times 78 = 78^4$

$45 \times 45 \times 45 \times 45 \times 45 = 45^5$

$2 \times 2 \times 2 \times 2 \times 2 \times 2 \times 2 \times 2 = 2^8$

$9^5 = 9 \times 9 \times 9 \times 9 \times 9$

$18^1 = 18$

$31^3 = 31 \times 31 \times 31$

$2^6 = 2 \times 2 \times 2 \times 2 \times 2 \times 2$

$55^2 = 55 \times 55$

$44^4 = 44 \times 44 \times 44 \times 44$

$72^5 = 72 \times 72 \times 72 \times 72 \times 72$

$8^6 = 8 \times 8 \times 8 \times 8 \times 8 \times 8$

PAGE 42

$4^2 = 4 \times 4 = 16$

$7^2 = 7 \times 7 = 49$

$10^3 = 10 \times 10 \times 10 = 1,000$

$12^2 = 12 \times 12 = 144$

$8^1 = 8$

$9^3 = 9 \times 9 \times 9 = 729$

$11^2 = 11 \times 11 = 121$

$17^2 = 17 \times 17 = 289$

64 > 16	9 = 9	125 > 100
169 > 26	196 < 343	64 = 64

PAGE 43

Exponents with 10			
10^1	10	10	1 zero
10^2	10 × 10	100	2 zeros
10^3	10 × 10 × 10	1,000	3 zeros
10^4	10 × 10 × 10 × 10	10,000	4 zeros
10^5	10 × 10 × 10 × 10 × 10	100,000	5 zeros
10^6	10 × 10 × 10 × 10 × 10 × 10	1,000, 000	6 zeros

$10^7 = 10,000,000$

$10^8 = 100,000,000$

$10^9 = 1,000,000,000$

$10^{10} = 10,000,000,000$

10^{32} will have 32 zeros. 10^{91} will have 91 zeros.

PAGE 44

4	13
11	37
30	29

PAGE 45

2	12
6	50
77	75
95	6

PAGE 46

5 < 9

33 > 23

29 > 10

5 = 5

78 < 154

PAGE 47

25	36
8	1

PAGE 48

14	2
4	21
24	23
3	10

PAGE 49

50 – 10

3 × (15 + 1)

7 – 3 + 5

2 × 12 – 2

3 × 6 + 2 × 12

2 × (16 – 8)

PAGE 50

D 2 × 12 + 5	E (12 – 2) ÷ 5
F (2 + 1) × 3	A (8 + 4) × 2
B 8 – 2 + 4	C 2 × 3 + 1

PAGE 51

6 × 5 + 2 × 2 = 34 hours

4 × 20 + 16 + 32 = $128

187 – 67 – 20 = 100 miles

28 ÷ 4 + 35 ÷ 5 = 14 desserts

PAGE 52

$t = 44$	$y = 60$	$m = 7$
$p = 371$	$r = 25$	$x = 192$
$b = 43$	$q = 573$	$a = 1,710$
$n = 4,601$	$f = 8,556$	$w = 57$

PAGE 53

$h = 80$	$j = 4$	$s = 175$
$p = 327$	$c = 336$	$z = 166$
$g = 548$	$u = 310$	$d = 181$

PAGE 54

$t = 20$	$h = 8$
$m = 20$	$y = 6$

PAGE 55

0.26	0.6
1.07	1.4

PAGE 55, continued

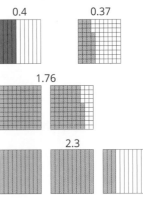

0.4   0.37

1.76

2.3

PAGE 56

0.⑥5	5.①9	8.⑥	112.⑧3
1.4⑧	62.9④	0.5⑧2	78.1⓪3
5.29④1	14.49①	6.82⑦8	
77.14⑧	12.84⑧1	0.48②9	

PAGE 57

Answers may vary. Some possible answers are shown below.

0.40 = 0.4   6.1 = 6.10

32.30 = 32.3   40.99 = 40.990

58.700 = 58.70 = 58.7

3.59 = 3.590 = 3.5900

0.220 = 0.22 = 0.2200

PAGE 58

5.31 > 5.30

4.65 < 4.66

17.1 > 1.71

24.84 > 24.48

25.91 < 26.19

3.10 = 3.1

15.05 < 15.5

29.4 > 2.94

11.1 > 11.01

PAGE 59

2.08	2.1	2.17	
4.65	46.5	146.5	
3.71	37.71	303.17	
2.909	2.919	2.991	
6.25	6.254	6.524	64.52
11.5	11.58	15.81	15.818

Answer key

PAGE 60

15	25	11	454
4.9	211.3	17.1	235.8
26.07	88.90	61.49	221.39
0.481	2.387	91.091	1.004

PAGE 61

$$\begin{array}{r} 4.85 \\ +\ 1.34 \\ \hline 6.19 \end{array} \qquad \begin{array}{r} 47.6 \\ +13.5 \\ \hline 61.1 \end{array} \qquad \begin{array}{r} 62.9 \\ +\ 8.3 \\ \hline 71.2 \end{array}$$

$$\begin{array}{r} 29.36 \\ +73.61 \\ \hline 102.97 \end{array} \qquad \begin{array}{r} 9.89 \\ +\ 0.57 \\ \hline 10.46 \end{array} \qquad \begin{array}{r} 16.71 \\ +24.43 \\ \hline 41.14 \end{array}$$

$$\begin{array}{r} 93.33 \\ +52.47 \\ \hline 145.80 \end{array} \qquad \begin{array}{r} 60.72 \\ +35.41 \\ \hline 96.13 \end{array} \qquad \begin{array}{r} 24.61 \\ +77.38 \\ \hline 101.99 \end{array}$$

$$\begin{array}{r} 120.17 \\ +372.07 \\ \hline 492.24 \end{array} \qquad \begin{array}{r} 255.08 \\ +\ 95.35 \\ \hline 350.43 \end{array}$$

PAGE 62

13.6 + 5.86 = 19.46
29 + 2.64 = 31.64

19.74 + 8.9 = 28.64
0.8 + 0.97 = 1.77

3.1 + 71.42 = 74.52
17.39 + 5.2 = 22.59

54.5 + 116.76 = 171.26
43.68 + 5.7 = 49.38

86.8 + 4.63 = 91.43
254.32 + 8.89 = 263.21

99.85 + 37.2 = 137.05
84.3 + 63.96 = 148.26

PAGE 63

$$\begin{array}{r} 27.06 \\ -16.94 \\ \hline 10.12 \end{array} \qquad \begin{array}{r} 3.31 \\ -2.08 \\ \hline 1.23 \end{array} \qquad \begin{array}{r} 81.83 \\ -42.32 \\ \hline 39.51 \end{array}$$

$$\begin{array}{r} 67.12 \\ -29.43 \\ \hline 37.69 \end{array} \qquad \begin{array}{r} 8.11 \\ -7.19 \\ \hline 0.92 \end{array} \qquad \begin{array}{r} 8.43 \\ -3.67 \\ \hline 4.76 \end{array}$$

$$\begin{array}{r} 92.59 \\ -\ 7.17 \\ \hline 85.42 \end{array} \qquad \begin{array}{r} 49.92 \\ -15.99 \\ \hline 33.93 \end{array} \qquad \begin{array}{r} 68.21 \\ -11.59 \\ \hline 56.62 \end{array}$$

PAGE 63, *continued*

$$\begin{array}{r} 46.14 \\ -\ 8.88 \\ \hline 37.26 \end{array} \qquad \begin{array}{r} 153.84 \\ -147.91 \\ \hline 5.93 \end{array}$$

PAGE 64

18.46 – 12.9 = 5.56
24.67 – 15 = 9.67

36.4 – 12.25 = 24.15
110.12 – 97.6 = 12.52

82.5 – 48.94 = 33.56
49.68 – 9.8 = 39.88

81.08 – 8.6 = 72.48
200 – 39.44 = 160.56

PAGE 65

12.17 – 9.68 = 2.49
5.8 + 8.35 = 14.15

9.55 – 8.8 = 0.75
76.3 – 34.59 = 41.71

73.5 + 9.96 = 83.46
6.36 + 13.9 = 20.26

83 – 20.6 = 62.4
76.7 + 3.47 = 80.17

83.13 + 72.8 = 155.93
130.58 – 7.6 = 122.98

87.6 + 49.99 = 137.59

PAGE 66

$7.20
$1.60
$7.50
$3.29

PAGE 67

$$\begin{array}{r} 8.3 \\ \times\ 5 \\ \hline 41.5 \end{array} \qquad \begin{array}{r} 6.7 \\ \times\ 8 \\ \hline 53.6 \end{array} \qquad \begin{array}{r} 16.4 \\ \times\ 3 \\ \hline 49.2 \end{array}$$

$$\begin{array}{r} 2.59 \\ \times\ 4 \\ \hline 10.36 \end{array} \qquad \begin{array}{r} 74.26 \\ \times\ 7 \\ \hline 519.82 \end{array} \qquad \begin{array}{r} 380.9 \\ \times\ 9 \\ \hline 3,428.1 \end{array}$$

PAGE 68

$$\begin{array}{r} 2.5 \\ \times\ 61 \\ \hline 152.5 \end{array} \qquad \begin{array}{r} 8.2 \\ \times\ 19 \\ \hline 155.8 \end{array} \qquad \begin{array}{r} 4.6 \\ \times\ 72 \\ \hline 331.2 \end{array}$$

$$\begin{array}{r} 5.3 \\ \times\ 87 \\ \hline 461.1 \end{array} \qquad \begin{array}{r} 3.4 \\ \times\ 58 \\ \hline 197.2 \end{array} \qquad \begin{array}{r} 0.49 \\ \times\ 37 \\ \hline 18.13 \end{array}$$

$$\begin{array}{r} 4.3 \\ \times\ 94 \\ \hline 404.2 \end{array} \qquad \begin{array}{r} 0.16 \\ \times\ 52 \\ \hline 8.32 \end{array} \qquad \begin{array}{r} 39.3 \\ \times\ 81 \\ \hline 3,183.3 \end{array}$$

$$\begin{array}{r} 6.04 \\ \times\ 26 \\ \hline 157.04 \end{array} \qquad \begin{array}{r} 72.5 \\ \times\ 98 \\ \hline 7,105.0 \end{array} \qquad \begin{array}{r} 5.69 \\ \times\ 57 \\ \hline 324.33 \end{array}$$

PAGE 69

72.24 × 4 = 288.96
8.214 × 3 = 24.642

6.8 × 32 = 217.6
9.3 × 24 = 223.2

74 × 4.7 = 347.8
61 × 0.28 = 17.08

18.6 × 52 = 967.2
209 × 1.9 = 397.1

PAGE 70

16.3 × 1 = 16.3
16.3 × 10 = 163
16.3 × 100 = 1,630
16.3 × 1,000 = 16,300
16.3 × 10,000 = 163,000

5.05 × 1 = 5.05
5.05 × 10 = 50.5
5.05 × 100 = 505
5.05 × 1,000 = 5,050
5.05 × 10,000 = 50,500

7.025 × 1 = 7.025
7.025 × 10 = 70.25
7.025 × 100 = 702.5
7.025 × 1,000 = 7,025
7.025 × 10,000 = 70,250

65.38 × 1 = 65.38
65.38 × 10 = 653.8
65.38 × 100 = 6,538
65.38 × 1,000 = 65,380
65.38 × 10,000 = 653,800

PAGE 71

1.94 × 10 = 19.4

2.5 × 100 = 250

6.88 × 100 = 688

0.99 × 10 = 9.9

42.1 × 1,000 = 42,100

1.36 × 1,000 = 1,360

5.7 × 1,000 = 5,700

0.112 × 100 = 11.2

2.9 × 10,000 = 29,000

14.8 × 1,000 = 14,800

0.2 × 100,000 = 20,000

9.3 × 10,000 = 93,000

1.364 × 1,000 = 1,364

0.17 × 100,000 = 17,000

PAGE 72

$3.9 \times 10^3 = 3,900$

$3.9 \times 10^4 = 39,000$

$8.1 \times 10^0 = 8.1$

$8.1 \times 10^1 = 81$

$8.1 \times 10^2 = 810$

$8.1 \times 10^3 = 8,100$

$8.1 \times 10^4 = 81,000$

$0.46 \times 10^0 = 0.46$

$0.46 \times 10^1 = 4.6$

$0.46 \times 10^2 = 46$

$0.46 \times 10^3 = 460$

$0.46 \times 10^4 = 4,600$

PAGE 73

$54.06 \times 10^1 = 540.6$

$44.31 \times 10^2 = 4,431$

$21.4 \times 10^4 = 214,000$

$9.049 \times 10^3 = 9,049$

$7.823 \times 10^5 = 782,300$

$315.77 \times 10^3 = 315,770$

$88.456 \times 10^6 = 88,456,000$

$529.8 \times 10^6 = 529,800,000$

$1.52 \times 10^7 = 15,200,000$

$2.4 \times 10^8 = 240,000,000$

$0.1 \times 10^9 = 100,000,000$

$0.33 \times 10^8 = 33,000,000$

PAGE 74

3.6	8.1	9.6
× 0.3	× 0.6	× 0.4
1.08	4.86	3.84

2.35	7.28	4.75
× 0.2	× 0.5	× 0.8
0.47	3.64	3.8

PAGE 75

5.3	6.3	4.5
× 2.4	× 6.3	× 2.1
12.72	39.69	9.45

9.7	0.64	9.9
× 8.6	× 3.7	× 9.9
83.42	2.368	98.01

3.02	5.96	2.88
× 1.4	× 2.2	× 4.6
4.228	13.112	13.248

8.24	7.65	9.89
× 1.7	× 3.3	× 5.8
14.008	25.245	57.362

PAGE 76

9.75 × 0.3 = 2.925   0.5 × 19.2 = (9.6)

46.4 × 0.4 = 18.56   3.2 × 1.8 = 5.76

1.5 × 6.4 = (9.6)   8.8 × 7.9 = 69.52

3.08 × 0.32 = 0.9856   0.25 × 38.4 = (9.6)

PAGE 77

$29.90

58.75 inches

$3.45

20.4 pounds

PAGE 78

1.55 miles

2.25 miles

69.3 miles

9.3 miles

PAGE 79

3)13.5 = 4.5   6)95.4 = 15.9   4)1.28 = 0.32

9)218.7 = 24.3   11)41.8 = 3.8   14)869.4 = 62.1

PAGE 80

5)9.30 = 1.86   6)34.50 = 5.75   8)113.20 = 14.15

12)24.60 = 2.05   16)178.40 = 11.15   24)217.20 = 9.05

PAGE 81

9)11.61 = 1.29   8)72.40 = 9.05   11)81.4 = 7.4

16)76.96 = 4.81   21)115.5 = 5.5   15)48.30 = 3.22

12)61.80 = 5.15   14)46.06 = 3.29   25)200.50 = 8.02

22)74.36 = 3.38   36)223.2 = 6.2

PAGE 82

7.4 ÷ 1 = 7.4

7.4 ÷ 10 = 0.74

7.4 ÷ 100 = 0.074

7.4 ÷ 1,000 = 0.0074

7.4 ÷ 10,000 = 0.00074

33.89 ÷ 1 = 33.89

33.89 ÷ 10 = 3.389

33.89 ÷ 100 = 0.3389

33.89 ÷ 1,000 = 0.03389

33.89 ÷ 10,000 = 0.003389

2.53 ÷ 1 = 2.53

2.53 ÷ 10 = 0.253

2.53 ÷ 100 = 0.0253

2.53 ÷ 1,000 = 0.00253

2.53 ÷ 10,000 = 0.000253

0.9 ÷ 1 = 0.9

0.9 ÷ 10 = 0.09

0.9 ÷ 100 = 0.009

0.9 ÷ 1,000 = 0.0009

0.9 ÷ 10,000 = 0.00009

PAGE 83

8.6 ÷ 10 = 0.86

5.14 ÷ 100 = 0.0514

445.1 ÷ 100 = 4.451

52.3 ÷ 1,000 = 0.0523

8 ÷ 100 = 0.08

9.2 ÷ 1,000 = 0.0092

PAGE 83, *continued*

0.76 ÷ 100 = 0.0076

52.7 ÷ 10,000 = 0.00527

1.28 ÷ 1,000 = 0.00128

3 ÷ 10,000 = 0.0003

0.4 ÷ 100,000 = 0.000004

1.7 ÷ 100,000 = 0.000017

Yes. You can move the decimal point to the left based on the exponent.

$1.7 ÷ 10^6 = 0.0000017$

$1.7 ÷ 10^7 = 0.00000017$

PAGE 84

$0.6 \overline{)8.82}$ = 14.7 $0.4 \overline{)4.48}$ = 11.2 $0.7 \overline{)12.81}$ = 18.3

$1.1 \overline{)3.85}$ = 3.5 $1.2 \overline{)29.52}$ = 24.6 $1.7 \overline{)43.86}$ = 25.8

PAGE 85

$1.9 \overline{)9.31}$ = 4.9 $1.2 \overline{)7.620}$ = 6.35 $2.1 \overline{)90.51}$ = 43.1

$1.8 \overline{)4.050}$ = 2.25 $3.3 \overline{)269.94}$ = 81.8 $4.1 \overline{)115.62}$ = 28.2

$3.4 \overline{)25.50}$ = 7.5 $2.4 \overline{)81.84}$ = 34.1 $2.5 \overline{)55.700}$ = 22.28

$1.6 \overline{)13.200}$ = 8.25 $3.5 \overline{)165.90}$ = 47.4

PAGE 86

5.67 ÷ 0.3 = 18.9

40.6 ÷ 14 = 2.9

68.4 ÷ 9 = 7.6

7.08 ÷ 0.8 = 8.85

153.45 ÷ 33 = 4.65

32.24 ÷ 2.6 = 12.4

97.56 ÷ 18 = 5.42

16.32 ÷ 1.7 = 9.6

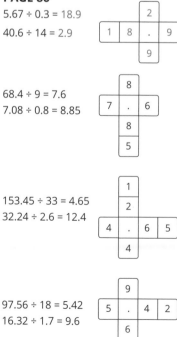

PAGE 87

3.65 inches

68.9 miles

$45.90

Green beans are $2.45 per pound. Asparagus is $2.90 per pound. So, green beans are cheaper per pound.

PAGE 88

$8 \overline{)44.0}$ = 5.5 $16 \overline{)68.00}$ = 4.25 $50 \overline{)25.0}$ = 0.5

PAGE 89

2.5 ounces

$8.75

0.2 pounds

0.75 ounces

PAGE 90

$\frac{1}{6}$ $\frac{4}{12}$ or $\frac{1}{3}$ $\frac{7}{10}$

$\frac{3}{6}$ or $\frac{1}{2}$ $\frac{3}{7}$ $\frac{2}{8}$ or $\frac{1}{4}$

$\frac{2}{5}$

$\frac{4}{8}$ or $\frac{1}{2}$

PAGE 91

Placement of shading may vary.

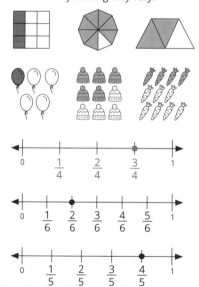

PAGE 92

Answers may vary. Some possible answers are shown below.

$\frac{7}{8} = \frac{14}{16}$ $\frac{3}{12} = \frac{1}{4}$

$\frac{2}{3} = \frac{4}{6}$ $\frac{3}{5} = \frac{6}{10}$

$\frac{4}{10} = \frac{2}{5}$ $\frac{4}{7} = \frac{8}{14}$

$\frac{7}{11} = \frac{14}{22}$ $\frac{3}{9} = \frac{1}{3}$

$\frac{10}{12} = \frac{5}{6}$ $\frac{4}{9} = \frac{8}{18}$

Other possible answers are shown below.

$\frac{21}{24}$ $\frac{6}{24}$

$\frac{6}{9}$ $\frac{9}{15}$

$\frac{8}{20}$ $\frac{12}{21}$

$\frac{21}{33}$ $\frac{6}{18}$

$\frac{20}{24}$ $\frac{12}{27}$

PAGE 93

Factors of 2: 1, ②
Factors of 6: 1, ②, 3, 6 $\frac{2}{6} = \frac{1}{3}$

Factors of 4: 1, 2, ④
Factors of 16: 1, 2, ④, 8, 16 $\frac{4}{16} = \frac{1}{4}$

Factors of 10: 1, 2, ⑤, 10
Factors of 15: 1, 3, ⑤, 15 $\frac{10}{15} = \frac{2}{3}$

PAGE 94

$\frac{5}{35} = \frac{1}{7}$ $\frac{14}{20} = \frac{7}{10}$ $\frac{22}{24} = \frac{11}{12}$

$\frac{8}{64} = \frac{1}{8}$ $\frac{11}{55} = \frac{1}{5}$ $\frac{5}{60} = \frac{1}{12}$

$\frac{16}{24} = \frac{2}{3}$ $\frac{12}{48} = \frac{1}{4}$ $\frac{27}{63} = \frac{3}{7}$

$\frac{25}{45} = \frac{5}{9}$ $\frac{36}{40} = \frac{9}{10}$ $\frac{18}{30} = \frac{3}{5}$

$\frac{24}{60} = \frac{2}{5}$ $\frac{15}{33} = \frac{5}{11}$ $\frac{20}{35} = \frac{4}{7}$

$\frac{10}{100} = \frac{1}{10}$ $\frac{45}{63} = \frac{5}{7}$

PAGE 95

Fraction	Equivalent fraction	Decimal
$\frac{1}{5}$	$\frac{2}{10}$	0.2
$\frac{41}{50}$	$\frac{82}{100}$	0.82
$\frac{11}{20}$	$\frac{55}{100}$	0.55
$\frac{1}{2}$	$\frac{5}{10}$	0.5
$\frac{27}{50}$	$\frac{54}{100}$	0.54
$\frac{17}{25}$	$\frac{68}{100}$	0.68

PAGE 96

$\frac{3}{5} = 0.6$ $\frac{1}{4} = 0.25$ $\frac{2}{25} = 0.08$

$\frac{1}{10} = 0.1$ $\frac{33}{50} = 0.66$ $\frac{7}{100} = 0.07$

$\frac{4}{5} = 0.8$ $\frac{3}{20} = 0.15$ $\frac{9}{10} = 0.9$

$\frac{19}{20} = 0.95$ $\frac{3}{10} = 0.3$ $\frac{43}{100} = 0.43$

$\frac{24}{25} = 0.96$ $\frac{2}{5} = 0.4$ $\frac{17}{20} = 0.85$

$\frac{18}{50} = 0.36$ $\frac{14}{25} = 0.56$ $\frac{47}{50} = 0.94$

PAGE 97

$0.87 = \frac{87}{100}$ $0.6 = \frac{3}{5}$

$0.8 = \frac{4}{5}$ $0.51 = \frac{51}{100}$

$0.9 = \frac{9}{10}$ $0.75 = \frac{3}{4}$

$0.16 = \frac{4}{25}$ $0.01 = \frac{1}{100}$

$0.2 = \frac{1}{5}$ $0.58 = \frac{29}{50}$

PAGE 98

$0.5 < \frac{3}{4}$ $0.23 > \frac{1}{5}$ $\frac{90}{100} > 0.29$

$0.63 > \frac{1}{2}$ $\frac{7}{10} < 0.8$ $0.81 > \frac{8}{10}$

$\frac{1}{4} > 0.19$ $0.55 < \frac{6}{10}$ $\frac{1}{25} = 0.04$

$\frac{25}{50} > 0.25$ $0.4 = \frac{8}{20}$ $\frac{16}{20} < 0.85$

$\frac{3}{5} = 0.6$ $\frac{3}{100} < 0.3$ $0.95 < \frac{24}{25}$

PAGE 99

80%   6%   63%

100%   47%

PAGE 100

0.26   0.12   0.05   0.40
0.01   0.76   0.22   1.00
0.89   0.20   0.17   0.71
0.93   0.35   0.49   0.06

PAGE 101

90%   4%   23%   60%
91%   77%   1%   84%
100%   50%   73%   16%
65%   81%   29%   30%

PAGE 102

75%

85%

PAGE 103

50%

20%

30%

86%

PAGE 104

$\frac{5}{9} + \frac{1}{9} = \frac{2}{3}$ $\frac{7}{8} - \frac{3}{8} = \frac{1}{2}$

$\frac{9}{10} - \frac{3}{10} = \frac{3}{5}$ $\frac{1}{3} + \frac{1}{3} = \frac{2}{3}$

$\frac{4}{11} + \frac{6}{11} = \frac{10}{11}$ $\frac{11}{12} - \frac{7}{12} = \frac{1}{3}$

$\frac{6}{7} - \frac{5}{7} = \frac{1}{7}$ $\frac{14}{15} - \frac{11}{15} = \frac{1}{5}$

$\frac{3}{16} + \frac{3}{16} = \frac{3}{8}$ $\frac{13}{14} - \frac{1}{14} = \frac{6}{7}$

$\frac{7}{12} - \frac{1}{12} = \frac{1}{2}$

PAGE 105

$\frac{2}{3} + \frac{1}{4} = \frac{11}{12}$ $\frac{1}{5} + \frac{3}{10} = \frac{1}{2}$
$\downarrow \quad \downarrow$ $\downarrow \quad \downarrow$
$\frac{8}{12} + \frac{3}{12}$ $\frac{2}{10} + \frac{3}{10}$

$\frac{1}{2} + \frac{2}{7} = \frac{11}{14}$ $\frac{1}{6} + \frac{2}{9} = \frac{7}{18}$
$\downarrow \quad \downarrow$ $\downarrow \quad \downarrow$
$\frac{7}{14} + \frac{4}{14}$ $\frac{3}{18} + \frac{4}{18}$

PAGE 106

$\frac{1}{4} + \frac{1}{6} = \frac{5}{12}$ $\frac{1}{2} + \frac{2}{9} = \frac{13}{18}$

$\frac{3}{8} + \frac{1}{6} = \frac{13}{24}$ $\frac{3}{4} + \frac{1}{12} = \frac{5}{6}$

$\frac{1}{10} + \frac{1}{4} = \frac{7}{20}$ $\frac{2}{3} + \frac{1}{8} = \frac{19}{24}$

$\frac{1}{3} + \frac{2}{5} = \frac{11}{15}$ $\frac{3}{5} + \frac{2}{7} = \frac{31}{35}$

$\frac{5}{12} + \frac{3}{8} = \frac{19}{24}$ $\frac{2}{11} + \frac{3}{4} = \frac{41}{44}$

PAGE 107

$\frac{4}{5} - \frac{2}{3} = \frac{2}{15}$ $\frac{3}{4} - \frac{1}{2} = \frac{1}{4}$

$\frac{11}{12} - \frac{5}{6} = \frac{1}{12}$ $\frac{3}{5} - \frac{1}{4} = \frac{7}{20}$

$\frac{6}{7} - \frac{1}{3} = \frac{11}{21}$ $\frac{9}{10} - \frac{2}{5} = \frac{1}{2}$

$\frac{5}{6} - \frac{3}{8} = \frac{11}{24}$ $\frac{3}{4} - \frac{3}{7} = \frac{9}{28}$

PAGE 108

$\frac{1}{5} + \frac{3}{7} = \frac{22}{35}$ $\frac{4}{5} - \frac{1}{4} = \frac{11}{20}$

$\frac{1}{9} + \frac{2}{3} = \frac{7}{9}$ $\frac{8}{11} - \frac{1}{2} = \frac{5}{22}$

$\frac{5}{6} - \frac{4}{7} = \frac{11}{42}$ $\frac{1}{10} + \frac{2}{5} = \frac{1}{2}$

$\frac{3}{8} + \frac{1}{3} = \frac{17}{24}$ $\frac{8}{9} - \frac{3}{4} = \frac{5}{36}$

$\frac{5}{6} - \frac{1}{8} = \frac{17}{24}$ $\frac{3}{10} + \frac{7}{12} = \frac{53}{60}$

PAGE 109

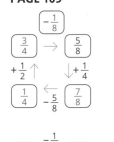

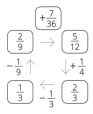

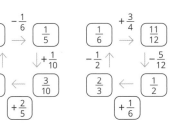

Answer key

PAGE 110

$\frac{7}{8}$ of a teaspoon

$\frac{5}{21}$

$\frac{7}{10}$ full

$\frac{1}{12}$ of a gallon

PAGE 111

$2\frac{1}{3} = \frac{7}{3}$

$3\frac{5}{6} = \frac{23}{6}$

$2\frac{3}{8} = \frac{19}{8}$

$1\frac{3}{4} = \frac{7}{4}$

$3\frac{2}{3} = \frac{11}{3}$

$2\frac{11}{12} = \frac{35}{12}$

Answers may vary. One possible answer is shown below.

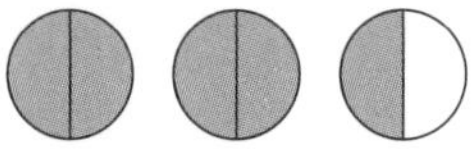

PAGE 112

$2\frac{1}{6} = \frac{13}{6}$ $1\frac{2}{3} = \frac{5}{3}$ $2\frac{3}{5} = \frac{13}{5}$

$1\frac{1}{9} = \frac{10}{9}$ $3\frac{3}{4} = \frac{15}{4}$ $2\frac{4}{7} = \frac{18}{7}$

$1\frac{9}{10} = \frac{19}{10}$ $2\frac{5}{6} = \frac{17}{6}$ $3\frac{2}{9} = \frac{29}{9}$

$2\frac{7}{8} = \frac{23}{8}$ $3\frac{5}{12} = \frac{41}{12}$ $3\frac{10}{11} = \frac{43}{11}$

Answers may vary. One possible answer is shown below.

To convert mixed numbers to improper fractions, multiply the whole number by the denominator, and then add the numerator. Write this new numerator over the original denominator.

PAGE 113

$\frac{10}{8} = 1\frac{1}{4}$ $\frac{9}{4} = 2\frac{1}{4}$

$\frac{13}{7} = 1\frac{6}{7}$ $\frac{9}{6} = 1\frac{1}{2}$

$\frac{14}{4} = 3\frac{1}{2}$ $\frac{13}{5} = 2\frac{3}{5}$

$\frac{35}{10} = 3\frac{1}{2}$ $\frac{31}{11} = 2\frac{9}{11}$

$\frac{25}{7} = 3\frac{4}{7}$ $\frac{46}{12} = 3\frac{5}{6}$

$\frac{24}{9} = 2\frac{2}{3}$

Answers may vary. One possible answer is shown below.

To convert improper fractions to mixed numbers, divide the numerator by the denominator. Then write the remainder as a fraction over the original denominator.

PAGE 114

$5\frac{1}{5} + 3\frac{1}{4} = 8\frac{9}{20}$ $6 + 1\frac{1}{5} = 7\frac{1}{5}$

$8\frac{1}{9} + 1\frac{2}{9} = 9\frac{1}{3}$ $2\frac{3}{10} + 4\frac{2}{5} = 6\frac{7}{10}$

$3\frac{7}{12} + \frac{1}{4} = 3\frac{5}{6}$ $6\frac{1}{6} + 4\frac{2}{5} = 10\frac{17}{30}$

PAGE 115

$4\frac{2}{3} + 2\frac{3}{4} = 7\frac{5}{12}$ $7\frac{11}{12} + \frac{7}{12} = 8\frac{1}{2}$

$3\frac{1}{2} + 1\frac{5}{8} = 5\frac{1}{8}$ $5\frac{3}{4} + 3\frac{5}{6} = 9\frac{7}{12}$

$4\frac{1}{3} + 4\frac{5}{7} = 9\frac{1}{21}$ $8\frac{9}{10} + 3\frac{1}{4} = 12\frac{3}{20}$

PAGE 116

$3\frac{1}{8} + 3\frac{1}{6} = 6\frac{7}{24}$ $7\frac{6}{7} + 4 = 11\frac{6}{7}$

$2\frac{1}{2} + 6\frac{5}{9} = 9\frac{1}{18}$ $5\frac{2}{3} + 8\frac{1}{4} = 13\frac{11}{12}$

$9\frac{4}{11} + \frac{4}{5} = 10\frac{9}{55}$ $4\frac{7}{10} + 3\frac{7}{10} = 8\frac{2}{5}$

$\frac{5}{8} + 11\frac{3}{4} = 12\frac{3}{8}$ $2\frac{3}{7} + 10\frac{2}{9} = 12\frac{41}{63}$

$7\frac{7}{10} + 9\frac{3}{8} = 17\frac{3}{40}$

PAGE 117

$6\frac{4}{5} - 2\frac{1}{3} = 4\frac{7}{15}$ $7\frac{9}{10} - 2\frac{3}{10} = 5\frac{3}{5}$

$5\frac{5}{6} - 3\frac{1}{2} = 2\frac{1}{3}$ $10\frac{7}{8} - 5\frac{1}{3} = 5\frac{13}{24}$

$9\frac{3}{4} - 6\frac{2}{9} = 3\frac{19}{36}$ $10\frac{11}{12} - \frac{5}{8} = 10\frac{7}{24}$

PAGE 118

$4\frac{1}{4} - 1\frac{2}{3} = 2\frac{7}{12}$ $11\frac{1}{4} - \frac{3}{4} = 10\frac{1}{2}$

$7\frac{3}{8} - 1\frac{1}{2} = 5\frac{7}{8}$ $10 - 5\frac{4}{7} = 4\frac{3}{7}$

$8\frac{1}{6} - 2\frac{7}{12} = 5\frac{7}{12}$ $4\frac{1}{6} - 3\frac{5}{8} = \frac{13}{24}$

PAGE 119

$11\frac{1}{9} - 9\frac{7}{9} = 1\frac{1}{3}$ $6\frac{2}{5} - \frac{2}{3} = 5\frac{11}{15}$

$10\frac{1}{4} - 5\frac{5}{8} = 4\frac{5}{8}$ $8\frac{5}{6} - 6 = 2\frac{5}{6}$

$9\frac{3}{8} - 8\frac{1}{12} = 1\frac{7}{24}$ $7\frac{4}{7} - 3\frac{1}{2} = 4\frac{1}{14}$

$15\frac{3}{7} - 7\frac{4}{5} = 7\frac{22}{35}$ $12 - 4\frac{3}{4} = 7\frac{1}{4}$

$2\frac{1}{5} - \frac{8}{11} = 1\frac{26}{55}$

PAGE 120

$4\frac{1}{5} + 3\frac{7}{10} = 7\frac{9}{10}$ $8\frac{1}{6} - 5\frac{5}{6} = 2\frac{1}{3}$

$2\frac{4}{7} + 6 = 8\frac{4}{7}$ $10\frac{1}{2} - \frac{3}{5} = 9\frac{9}{10}$

$11\frac{11}{12} - \frac{2}{3} = 11\frac{1}{4}$ $6\frac{4}{7} + 5\frac{1}{2} = 12\frac{1}{14}$

$12\frac{5}{6} - 9\frac{2}{3} = 3\frac{1}{6}$ $10 - 3\frac{7}{12} = 6\frac{5}{12}$

$8\frac{4}{5} + 7\frac{3}{4} = 16\frac{11}{20}$ $9\frac{1}{3} - 2\frac{2}{5} = 6\frac{14}{15}$

$5\frac{8}{9} + 9\frac{1}{6} = 15\frac{1}{18}$

PAGE 121

$9\frac{3}{10}$

$5\frac{1}{2}$ $3\frac{4}{5}$

$3\frac{1}{5}$ $2\frac{3}{10}$ $1\frac{1}{2}$

$11\frac{1}{8}$

$5\frac{3}{8}$ $5\frac{3}{4}$

$3\frac{1}{8}$ $2\frac{1}{4}$ $3\frac{1}{2}$

$5\frac{11}{20}$

$2\frac{3}{10}$ $3\frac{1}{4}$

$\frac{4}{5}$ $1\frac{1}{2}$ $1\frac{3}{4}$

12

$5\frac{8}{15}$ $6\frac{7}{15}$

$1\frac{1}{5}$ $4\frac{1}{3}$ $2\frac{2}{15}$

$7\frac{17}{24}$

$3\frac{1}{4}$ $4\frac{11}{24}$

$\frac{5}{8}$ $2\frac{5}{8}$ $1\frac{5}{6}$

$8\frac{2}{5}$

$4\frac{1}{2}$ $3\frac{9}{10}$

$1\frac{5}{12}$ $3\frac{1}{12}$ $\frac{49}{60}$

PAGE 122

$2 \times \frac{3}{8} = \frac{3}{4}$ $3 \times \frac{1}{7} = \frac{3}{7}$

$8 \times \frac{1}{10} = \frac{4}{5}$ $\frac{1}{6} \times 3 = \frac{1}{2}$

$\frac{4}{5} \times 2 = 1\frac{3}{5}$ $2 \times \frac{5}{12} = \frac{5}{6}$

$9 \times \frac{3}{10} = 2\frac{7}{10}$ $\frac{3}{11} \times 8 = 2\frac{2}{11}$

$4 \times \frac{11}{12} = 3\frac{2}{3}$ $6 \times \frac{7}{8} = 5\frac{1}{4}$

PAGE 123

$7 \times \frac{1}{2} = 3\frac{1}{2}$ $8 \times \frac{1}{6} = 1\frac{1}{3}$

$9 \times \frac{3}{8} = 3\frac{3}{8}$ $\frac{11}{12} \times 5 = 4\frac{7}{12}$

$\frac{2}{3} \times 6 = 4$ $\frac{3}{4} \times 2 = 1\frac{1}{2}$

$4 \times \frac{7}{12} = 2\frac{1}{3}$ $3 \times \frac{5}{6} = 2\frac{1}{2}$

$\frac{3}{10} \times 6 = 1\frac{4}{5}$ $\frac{4}{5} \times 10 = 8$

$7 \times \frac{5}{9} = 3\frac{8}{9}$ $8 \times \frac{10}{11} = 7\frac{3}{11}$

$\frac{5}{6} \times 12 = 10$ $14 \times \frac{6}{7} = 12$

PAGE 124

$\frac{1}{6} \times \frac{2}{3} = \frac{1}{9}$ $\frac{5}{9} \times \frac{1}{3} = \frac{5}{27}$

$\frac{6}{7} \times \frac{1}{2} = \frac{3}{7}$ $\frac{3}{5} \times \frac{1}{2} = \frac{3}{10}$

$\frac{2}{5} \times \frac{7}{9} = \frac{14}{45}$ $\frac{2}{3} \times \frac{3}{8} = \frac{1}{4}$

$\frac{1}{4} \times \frac{5}{6} = \frac{5}{24}$ $\frac{1}{12} \times \frac{3}{4} = \frac{1}{16}$

$\frac{9}{10} \times \frac{2}{10} = \frac{9}{50}$ $\frac{9}{10} \times \frac{9}{10} = \frac{81}{100}$

$\frac{9}{10} \times \frac{9}{10}$ is equal to $\left(\frac{9}{10}\right)^2$.

PAGE 125

$\frac{3}{8} \times \frac{1}{2} = \frac{3}{16}$ $\frac{5}{7} \times \frac{1}{3} = \frac{5}{21}$

$\frac{3}{10} \times \frac{2}{3} = \frac{1}{5}$ $\frac{1}{4} \times \frac{1}{5} = \frac{1}{20}$

$\frac{1}{2} \times \frac{5}{12} = \frac{5}{24}$ $\frac{4}{5} \times \frac{2}{3} = \left(\frac{8}{15}\right)$

$\frac{3}{4} \times \frac{3}{4} = \left(\frac{9}{16}\right)$ $\frac{7}{9} \times \frac{1}{2} = \frac{7}{18}$

$\frac{5}{8} \times \frac{1}{4} = \frac{5}{32}$ $\frac{5}{9} \times \frac{3}{5} = \frac{1}{3}$

$\frac{7}{8} \times \frac{4}{5} = \left(\frac{7}{10}\right)$ $\frac{5}{11} \times \frac{11}{12} = \frac{5}{12}$

PAGE 126

$\frac{1}{8}$ of $6 = \frac{3}{4}$ $\frac{2}{3}$ of $4 = 2\frac{2}{3}$

$\frac{4}{9}$ of $3 = 1\frac{1}{3}$ $\frac{3}{4}$ of $8 = 6$

$\frac{1}{2}$ of $\frac{1}{5} = \frac{1}{10}$ $\frac{5}{6}$ of $\frac{1}{8} = \frac{5}{48}$

$\frac{2}{3}$ of $\frac{3}{7} = \frac{2}{7}$ $\frac{5}{12}$ of $\frac{3}{5} = \frac{1}{4}$

PAGE 127

4 signs

8 campers

$\frac{1}{4}$ of an hour

$\frac{1}{8}$

PAGE 128

$1\frac{1}{4} \times \frac{5}{6} = 1\frac{1}{24}$ $\frac{1}{5} \times 1\frac{1}{6} = \frac{7}{30}$

$4\frac{1}{2} \times \frac{3}{8} = 1\frac{11}{16}$ $3\frac{2}{3} \times \frac{3}{4} = 2\frac{3}{4}$

$3\frac{3}{4} \times \frac{3}{5} = 2\frac{1}{4}$ $\frac{5}{9} \times 2\frac{4}{5} = 1\frac{5}{9}$

$\frac{2}{3} \times 6\frac{1}{3} = 4\frac{2}{9}$

PAGE 129

$2\frac{1}{3} \times 2\frac{1}{2} = 5\frac{5}{6}$ $1\frac{1}{6} \times 3\frac{1}{2} = 4\frac{1}{12}$

$1\frac{1}{5} \times 1\frac{3}{4} = 2\frac{1}{10}$ $2\frac{2}{5} \times 1\frac{2}{7} = 3\frac{3}{35}$

$4\frac{1}{2} \times 2\frac{1}{3} = 10\frac{1}{2}$ $1\frac{1}{9} \times 1\frac{7}{8} = 2\frac{1}{12}$

$2\frac{5}{6} \times 3\frac{1}{2} = 9\frac{11}{12}$

PAGE 130

$4 \times \frac{3}{5} = 2\frac{2}{5}$ $\frac{1}{2} \times \frac{1}{3} = \frac{1}{6}$

$\frac{7}{8} \times \frac{1}{4} = \frac{7}{32}$ $\frac{5}{9} \times 5 = 2\frac{7}{9}$

$2\frac{1}{2} \times 3 = 7\frac{1}{2}$ $2\frac{1}{9} \times \frac{1}{4} = \frac{19}{36}$

$\frac{3}{5} \times 1\frac{2}{3} = 1$ $\frac{9}{10} \times 2\frac{1}{4} = 2\frac{1}{40}$

$3\frac{1}{5} \times 4 = 12\frac{4}{5}$ $4\frac{1}{2} \times 1\frac{3}{10} = 5\frac{17}{20}$

$1\frac{2}{7} \times 4\frac{1}{5} = 5\frac{2}{5}$

PAGE 131

START

$\frac{1}{4} \times 5$	$3\frac{1}{2} \times \frac{1}{3}$	$4 \times \frac{2}{5}$	$2\frac{1}{3} \times \frac{7}{8}$
$3\frac{1}{2} \times \frac{5}{6}$	$\frac{1}{2} \times \frac{1}{5}$	$1\frac{1}{8} \times 1\frac{1}{2}$	$2 \times \frac{1}{3}$
$5 \times \frac{3}{5}$	$\frac{7}{10} \times \frac{1}{4}$	$2\frac{1}{10} \times \frac{5}{7}$	$3\frac{3}{4} \times \frac{1}{8}$
$\frac{1}{2} \times \frac{6}{7}$	$1 \times 1\frac{1}{2}$	$\frac{3}{8} \times 3$	$4 \times \frac{5}{8}$
$1\frac{1}{2} \times 1\frac{2}{3}$	$4\frac{1}{5} \times \frac{2}{7}$	$\frac{7}{10} \times 5$	$\frac{7}{8} \times \frac{3}{4}$
$4\frac{1}{8} \times \frac{7}{10}$	$3 \times \frac{5}{12}$	$1\frac{1}{10} \times \frac{11}{12}$	$2\frac{1}{2} \times \frac{3}{5}$

FINISH

219

PAGE 132

$\frac{1}{4}$ of a teaspoon

$2\frac{1}{2}$ cups

1 teaspoon

$\frac{3}{4}$ of a cup

PAGE 133

9 miles

5 pounds

$1\frac{3}{4}$ cups

11 blocks

PAGE 134

$4 \times \frac{1}{9} = \frac{4}{9}$ The product is less than 4.

$4 \times 1\frac{1}{3} = 5\frac{1}{3}$ The product is greater than 4.

$4 \times 1 = 4$ The product is equal to 4.

If the second factor is less than 1, the product is less than the original number. If the second factor is greater than 1, the product is greater than the original number. If the second factor equals 1, the product equals the original number.

$10 \times 2\frac{4}{5} > 10$ $\frac{5}{6} \times \frac{1}{10} < \frac{5}{6}$

$9 \times \frac{2}{3} < 9$ $\frac{3}{5} \times 2\frac{1}{9} > \frac{3}{5}$

PAGE 135

$3 \div \frac{1}{3} = 9$

$4 \div \frac{1}{2} = 8$

$2 \div \frac{1}{4} = 8$

$3 \div \frac{1}{6} = 18$

PAGE 136

$\frac{1}{5} \div 2 = \frac{1}{10}$

$\frac{1}{3} \div 4 = \frac{1}{12}$

$\frac{1}{6} \div 3 = \frac{1}{18}$

$\frac{1}{4} \div 2 = \frac{1}{8}$

PAGE 137

$4 \div \frac{1}{5} = 20$ $\frac{1}{4} \div 5 = \frac{1}{20}$

$2 \div \frac{1}{6} = 12$ $\frac{1}{2} \div 6 = \frac{1}{12}$

$3 \div \frac{1}{5} = 15$ $\frac{1}{3} \div 5 = \frac{1}{15}$

$5 \div \frac{1}{2} = 10$ $\frac{1}{5} \div 2 = \frac{1}{10}$

PAGE 138

$\frac{1}{4}$ of a pound

14 days

$\frac{1}{12}$ of a pound

6 bandanas

PAGE 139

$\frac{4}{5} \rightarrow \frac{5}{4}$ $\frac{2}{9} \rightarrow \frac{9}{2}$ $\frac{10}{7} \rightarrow \frac{7}{10}$

$\frac{11}{12} \rightarrow \frac{12}{11}$ $4 \rightarrow \frac{1}{4}$ $\frac{5}{2} \rightarrow \frac{2}{5}$

$7 \rightarrow \frac{1}{7}$ $\frac{3}{4} \rightarrow \frac{4}{3}$ $\frac{1}{10} \rightarrow \frac{10}{1}$ or 10

$\frac{5}{6} \rightarrow \frac{6}{5}$ $\frac{1}{3} \rightarrow \frac{3}{1}$ or 3

PAGE 140

$\frac{3}{4} \div \frac{2}{3} = 1\frac{1}{8}$ $\frac{2}{5} \div \frac{1}{6} = 2\frac{2}{5}$

$\frac{6}{7} \div 3 = \frac{2}{7}$ $\frac{1}{4} \div \frac{8}{9} = \frac{9}{32}$

$\frac{5}{8} \div \frac{1}{2} = 1\frac{1}{4}$ $2 \div \frac{1}{3} = 6$

$\frac{9}{10} \div \frac{4}{5} = 1\frac{1}{8}$ $\frac{11}{12} \div 4 = \frac{11}{48}$

PAGE 141

$\frac{2}{9} \div \frac{1}{3} = \frac{2}{3}$ $\frac{1}{2} \div \frac{5}{7} = \frac{7}{10}$

$4 \div \frac{3}{4} = 5\frac{1}{3}$ $\frac{5}{6} \div \frac{1}{4} = 3\frac{1}{3}$

$\frac{3}{7} \div \frac{1}{5} = 2\frac{1}{7}$ $\frac{8}{9} \div 5 = \frac{8}{45}$

$8 \div \frac{2}{3} = 12$ $\frac{3}{10} \div \frac{1}{4} = 1\frac{1}{5}$

$\frac{3}{5} \div \frac{2}{7} = 2\frac{1}{10}$ $\frac{4}{9} \div \frac{2}{5} = 1\frac{1}{9}$

PAGE 142

$9 \div 6 = 1\frac{1}{2}$ $4 \div 22 = \frac{2}{11}$

$17 \div 7 = 2\frac{3}{7}$ $18 \div 8 = 2\frac{1}{4}$

$3 \div 36 = \frac{1}{12}$ $10 \div 12 = \frac{5}{6}$

$16 \div 40 = \frac{2}{5}$ $30 \div 9 = 3\frac{1}{3}$

$36 \div 27 = 1\frac{1}{3}$ $28 \div 6 = 4\frac{2}{3}$

$12 \div 42 = \frac{2}{7}$ $50 \div 16 = 3\frac{1}{8}$

PAGE 143

$\frac{1}{3}$ of a pound

$\frac{1}{4}$ of a pound

$\frac{3}{5}$ of a pound

$1\frac{1}{2}$ hours

$5\frac{1}{2}$ ounces

PAGE 144

Rule: subtract 12	87	75	63	51	39
Rule: add 9	10	19	28	37	46
Rule: multiply by 2	3	6	12	24	48
Rule: subtract 75	500	425	350	275	200
Rule: multiply by 3	1	3	9	27	81

PAGE 145

Rule: multiply by 2, then add 1	3	7	15	31	63
Rule: add 3, then multiply by 2	17	40	86	178	362
Rule: add 1, then multiply by 2	100	202	406	814	1,630
Rule: subtract 50, then multiply by 2	120	140	180	260	420
Rule: multiply by 3, then subtract 5	3	4	7	16	43
Rule: add 8, then multiply by 3	10	54	186	582	1,770
Rule: multiply by 2, then add 10	5	20	50	110	230

PAGE 146

Rule: add 0.8	1.1	1.9	2.7	3.5	4.3
Rule: subtract 2.5	20.3	17.8	15.3	12.8	10.3
Rule: add $\frac{1}{2}$	$\frac{1}{5}$	$\frac{7}{10}$	$1\frac{1}{5}$	$1\frac{7}{10}$	$2\frac{1}{5}$
Rule: subtract $\frac{1}{6}$	$\frac{11}{12}$	$\frac{3}{4}$	$\frac{7}{12}$	$\frac{5}{12}$	$\frac{1}{4}$
Rule: multiply by 0.5	100.8	50.4	25.2	12.6	6.3
Rule: multiply by $1\frac{1}{2}$	$1\frac{1}{3}$	2	3	$4\frac{1}{2}$	$6\frac{3}{4}$
Rule: add $1\frac{3}{4}$	$\frac{1}{6}$	$1\frac{11}{12}$	$3\frac{2}{3}$	$5\frac{5}{12}$	$7\frac{1}{6}$

PAGE 147

Rule: add 15	35	50	65	80	95
Rule: subtract 11	83	72	61	50	39
Rule: multiply by 4	1	4	16	64	256
Rule: multiply by 2	7	14	28	56	112
Rule: subtract 13	150	137	124	111	98
Rule: multiply by 5	3	15	75	375	1,875
Rule: add 111	111	222	333	444	555

PAGE 148

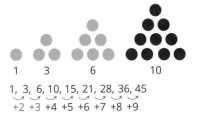

1, 3, 6, 10, 15, 21, 28, 36, 45
+2 +3 +4 +5 +6 +7 +8 +9

PAGE 149

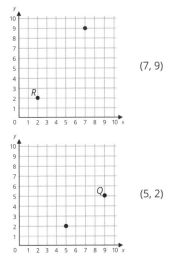

1, 4, 9, 16, 25, 36, 49, 64, 81, 100
+3 +5 +7 +9 +11 +13 +15 +17 +19

PAGE 151

A (1, 5)

B (3, 8)

C (7, 6)

D (9, 3)

E (2, 10)

F (3, 3)

PAGE 152

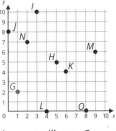

Answers will vary. One possible answer is shown below.

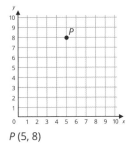

P (5, 8)

PAGE 153

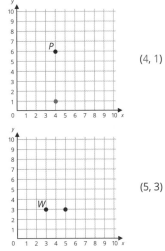

(4, 1)

(5, 3)

PAGE 153, *continued*

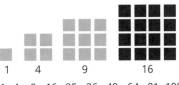

(7, 9)

(5, 2)

PAGE 154

5 units   3 units

6 units   8 units

PAGE 155

(10, 9)

Threads-R-Us Clothing Store

4 units

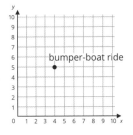

PAGE 156

(9, 6)

5 units

(6, 7)

PAGE 157

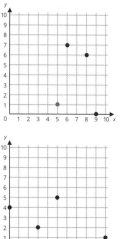

PAGE 158

6 pints

Saturday

Friday

Sunday

PAGE 159

$70

May

August

$100

PAGE 160

5 inches	7 feet
25 pounds	40 inches
30 feet	20 fluid ounces

| Length of a pen | Weight of a squirrel |
| Weight of a car | Height of a person |

PAGE 161

5 yd. = 15 ft.	36 in. = 3 ft.
24 ft. = 8 yd.	2 mi. = 3,520 yd.
$\frac{1}{2}$ ft. = 6 in.	$2\frac{1}{3}$ yd. = 7 ft.

PAGE 162

| 14 ft. = 4 yd. 2 ft. | 40 in. = 3 ft. 4 in. |
| 52 ft. = 17 yd. 1 ft. | 93 in. = 7 ft. 9 in. |

PAGE 163

2 lb. = 32 oz.

64 oz. = 4 lb.

6,000 lb. = 3 tons

20 oz. = 1 lb. 4 oz.

4 tons = 8,000 lb.

3,675 lb. = 1 ton 1,675 lb.

14 lb. = 224 oz.

35 oz. = 2 lb. 3 oz.

$\frac{1}{2}$ ton = 1,000 lb.

$5\frac{1}{2}$ lb. = 88 oz.

PAGE 164

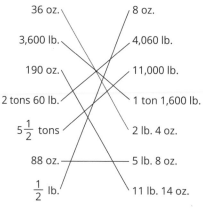

36 oz.	8 oz.
3,600 lb.	4,060 lb.
190 oz.	11,000 lb.
2 tons 60 lb.	1 ton 1,600 lb.
$5\frac{1}{2}$ tons	2 lb. 4 oz.
88 oz.	5 lb. 8 oz.
$\frac{1}{2}$ lb.	11 lb. 14 oz.

PAGE 165

16 c. = 8 pt.

4 c. = 32 fl. oz.

6 qt. = 1 gal. 2 qt.

5 gal. = 20 qt.

15 pt. = 7 qt. 1 pt.

27 fl. oz. = 3 c. 3 fl. oz.

$3\frac{1}{2}$ qt. = 7 pt.

$10\frac{1}{4}$ c. = 82 fl. oz.

27 qt. = 6 gal. 3 qt.

PAGE 166

| 144 fl. oz. = 18 c. | 26 pt. = 52 c. |
| $5\frac{1}{4}$ gal. = 21 qt. | 33 pt. = 16 qt. 1 pt. |

48 fl. oz. = 6 c. = 3 pt.

20 c. = 10 pt. = 5 qt.

6 pt. = 12 c. = 96 fl. oz.

11 gal. = 44 qt. = 88 pt. = 176 c.

96 c. = 48 pt. = 24 qt. = 6 gal.

PAGE 166, *continued*

To get from cups to gallons in one step, you would divide by 16, since there are 16 cups in 1 gallon.

PAGE 167

5 yards

12 cups

8 feet

12 pounds

PAGE 168

| 180 milliliters | 12 millimeters |
| 385 kilograms | 3 meters |

| Mass of a bowling ball | Length of a fork |
| Length of a bed | Capacity of a bathtub |

PAGE 169

2.2 m = 220 cm	19 mm = 1.9 cm
45 cm = 450 mm	6.4 km = 6,400 m
253 cm = 2.53 m	8.43 cm = 84.3 mm

PAGE 170

START				
3 km	300 m	8.1 m	810 cm	811 mm
3,000 m		81 cm		81.1 cm
74 mm	7.4 cm	5.4 m	0.54 km	6.05 cm
0.74 cm		540 cm		60.5 mm
15,000 m	1.5 km	3,570 m	357 km	74.2 km
15 km		3.57 km		74,200 m
12.5 mm	1.25 cm	436 mm	43.6 cm	FINISH

PAGE 171

8,400 mg = 8.4 g	3 kg = 3,000 g
7,100 g = 7.1 kg	9,750 mg = 9.75 g
1.2 kg = 1,200 g	50,000 g = 50 kg
24,300 mg = 24.3 g	3.3 g = 3,300 mg
15,770 g = 15.77 kg	

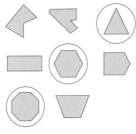

PAGE 172

25,000 mg = 25 g   3,700 mg = 3.7 g
2,500 g = 2.5 kg   3,700 g = 3.7 kg
2.5 g = 2,500 mg   3.07 g = 3,070 mg

12,400 g = 12.4 kg   5,100 mg = 5.1 g
12.4 g = 12,400 mg   51,000 g = 51 kg
1.24 g = 1,240 mg   51,000 mg = 51 g

1,890 g = 1.89 kg   65,000 g = 65 kg
1.89 g = 1,890 mg   6,500 mg = 6.5 g
18.9 kg = 18,900 g   650 g = 0.65 kg

PAGE 173

9,400 mL = 9.4 L   8.3 L = 8,300 mL
6.02 L = 6,020 mL   310 mL = 0.31 L
1,700 mL = 1.7 L   15.6 L = 15,600 mL
2.41 L = 2,410 mL   45,200 mL = 45.2 L
3,840 mL = 3.84 L

PAGE 174

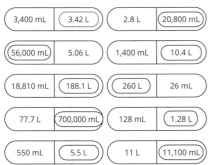

3,400 mL	3.42 L	2.8 L	20,800 mL
56,000 mL	5.06 L	1,400 mL	10.4 L
18,810 mL	188.1 L	260 L	26 mL
77.7 L	700,000 mL	128 mL	1.28 L
550 mL	5.5 L	11 L	11,100 mL

PAGE 175

7,200 mg < 720 g
7.3 cm = 73 mm
6,460 mL > 6.4 L
30 g > 3,000 mg
14,600 mg > 1.46 g
2.2 L = 2,200 mL
3,320 cm > 3.32 m
31.36 cm > 313 mm
805 mg < 80.5 g
52.2 km > 5,522 m

PAGE 176

350 milliliters
900 millimeters
1,200 grams
Pop's Bubbles

PAGE 177

6 hours 23 minutes
2 hours 44 minutes
4 hours 59 minutes
1 hour 55 minutes
2 hours 58 minutes
4 hours 28 minutes
2 hours 2 minutes

PAGE 178

1 hour 36 minutes
2 hours 17 minutes
4 hours 49 minutes
2 hours 42 minutes
1 hour 38 minutes

PAGE 179

12:55 p.m.
8:38 a.m.
1:42 p.m.
4:25 p.m.
10:16 a.m.

PAGE 180

3 hours 10 minutes
2 hours 37 minutes
9:21 a.m.

PAGE 181

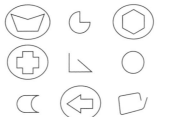

Answers will vary. One possible answer is shown below.

PAGE 182

quadrilateral   hexagon   pentagon
decagon   nonagon   heptagon

PAGE 183

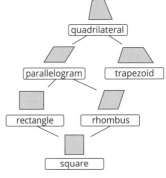

PAGE 184

straight   obtuse   acute
obtuse   acute   right
              right   obtuse

PAGE 185

perpendicular
neither
parallel

neither
perpendicular
neither

PAGE 186

acute   right   obtuse
acute   acute   obtuse

PAGE 187

equilateral   isosceles   scalene
isosceles   equilateral

PAGE 189

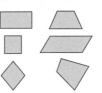

PAGE 190

Answers will vary. Some possible answers are shown below.

PAGE 191

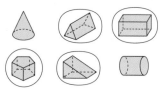

PAGE 192

pyramid	neither	prism
neither	pyramid	neither

PAGE 193

59 cm	72 in.
176.4 m	31.17 ft.
3 m	$7\frac{1}{2}$ ft.

To find the perimeter of that square, you can multiply $\frac{3}{4}$ by 4. To find the perimeter of that triangle, you can multiply $2\frac{1}{2}$ by 3.

PAGE 194

196 in.^{2}	390 yd.^{2}
94.8 mm^2	$\frac{3}{8}$ ft.^{2}
9 cm^2	20.25 m^2

PAGE 195

8 mm	8 in.
16 ft.	55 m
5 in.	19 mm
7 cm	

PAGE 196

4,484 square inches
576 square inches
314 feet
86.6 inches
18 feet

PAGE 197

27 units^3	60 units^3
12 units^3	30 units^3

PAGE 198

36 ft.^{3}	64 cm^3
50 m^3	168 in.^{3}

PAGE 199

343 mm^3	360 in.^{3}
90 m^3	210.9 cm.^{3}
$\frac{3}{4}$ ft.^{3}	

PAGE 200

167 ft.^{3}	520 cm^3

PAGE 201

280 m^3	157 ft.^{3}
1,728 cm^3	700 in.^{3}

PAGE 202

29 ounces

$\frac{1}{4}$ of a teaspoon

$\frac{1}{2}$ of a cup

$\frac{1}{2}$ of a tablespoon

PAGE 203

30 ounces
1.25 pounds
2 cups
$2\frac{3}{4}$ teaspoons
6 times

PAGE 204

12 hours 15 minutes
5 water aerobics classes
9 campers

PAGE 205

$3 \times 4 + 5 \times 3$
2,280 square feet
$3,410.00
161 feet

PAGE 206

$172.40
$12.21
114 square feet
$7,065
12 ornaments

PAGE 207

$90.00
360 cubic inches
6 feet
$342.50

PAGE 208

1.54 seconds
3.2 kilometers
3 hours 48 minutes
4,400 yards
3:40 p.m., 4:00 p.m., 4:20 p.m., 4:40 p.m., 5:00 p.m., and 5:20 p.m.

PAGE 209

75 inches
$19.98
(8, 1)
7 units